How to Get a First

You may also be interested in the following study titles
by Palgrave Macmillan:

For a complete listing of all titles in our Study Skills range please visit
www.palgrave.com/studyskills

How to Get a First

Insights and Advice from a First-class Graduate

Michael Tefula

palgrave
macmillan

First published 2012 by
PALGRAVE MACMILLAN
Palgrave Macmillan in the UK is an imprint of Macmillan Publishers Limited, registered in England, company number 785998, of Houndmills, Basingstoke,
Hampshire RG21 6XS.

Palgrave Macmillan in the US is a division of St Martin's Press LLC, 175 Fifth Avenue, New York, NY 10010.

Palgrave Macmillan is the global academic imprint of the above companies and has companies and representatives throughout the world.

Palgrave® and Macmillan® are registered trademarks in the United States, the United Kingdom, Europe and other countries

ISBN: 978–0-230–36220–8

This book is printed on paper suitable for recycling and made from fully managed and sustained forest sources. Logging, pulping and manufacturing processes are expected to conform to the environmental regulations of the country of origin.

A catalogue record for this book is available from the British Library.

A catalog record for this book is available from the Library of Congress.

10   9   8   7   6   5   4   3   2   1
21   20   19   18   17   16   15   14   13   12

Printed in China

Contents

Contents

Introduction

A valuable degree

In the academic year 2009/10, nearly half (48.2 per cent) of the students taking their first degree graduated with a 2:1. In contrast, only 14.3 per cent graduated with a first (HESA, 2011). If you settle for an average result, it will be increasingly hard to stand out. Upper second-class students are now in direct competition with half of their class and they are required to supplement their grades with work experience and extracurricular activities. Only then can students demonstrate to employers that they are 'well rounded' and worth taking an interest in.

But imagine if you were still a 'well rounded' student, took part in meaningful extracurricular activities, had plenty of work experience and, to top it all off, you graduated with a first-class degree. Isn't that the best possible combination? This would not only put you in the top 14.3 per cent of the student population, it would also place you in a smaller fraction of first-class students who are 'well rounded' and do not spend all of their life in a library. Becoming such a student would no doubt take a lot of work, but when student debt levels are expected to rise as high as £53,000 for students starting university in 2012 (Push, 2011), wouldn't you want to get the absolute best return on your investment? I hope your answer is a resounding 'yes', as in the coming chapters I will share with you tips and ideas that can help you achieve just that.

The purpose of this book

I will never forget the marks I received for my first piece of written coursework at university. The assignment was to write a 500-word précis (a summary of an academic journal article). When the results came back, the 55 per cent mark I received was somewhat unexpected – to be honest, it was a disappointment. As an AAB A-level student I thought I could do better. I had come to the University of Birmingham aiming for a first and now the reality had set in. I thought to myself, 'Getting a first is going to be the hardest thing you've ever done!'

Over the next three years I would experiment with memory techniques, time-management systems and all the revision methods I could get my hands on in order to improve my grades. I downloaded revision software, used stickers and flash cards, tried mind-mapping, and at one point even went as far as playing audio revision notes in my sleep! Some things worked, but unfortunately many didn't, and for my first two years I averaged a 2:1. In my third year, however, something clicked and I ended up graduating with a first-class degree. Looking back, I now realise that there were certain fundamentals that I took care of in my final year of university, without which all the study tips and strategies in the world could not be effective. So the main purpose of this book is to help you address these basic ingredients of academic success and to provide you with a range of ideas that can propel you to first-class results.

The format

The first part of this book is entitled 'The Fundamentals'. These are the key ideas that contribute greatly to how well you do at university. In total, there are five to consider: (1) Degree Choice, (2) The Growth Mindset, (3) Work Ethic, (4) Happiness and Grades, and (5) Support Systems. Without my knowing it, all of these building blocks had been taken care of by my final year and, as a result, I was able to improve my grades from a 2:1 to a first. I truly believe that if you too work on these areas as diligently as I did, then you will be on your way to a first-class degree. I am ever more certain of this because in writing this book I interviewed several other students who had achieved a first in various subject areas, from a range of universities including Warwick, Oxford and Manchester. It came as no surprise that they, too, had taken care of the majority of the fundamentals. (Snippets of some of these interviews will be available in various parts of the book.) OK, some of the basic elements I detail may initially appear abstract or fluffy – for example, you may be wondering what happiness has to do with grades – but rest assured, their importance will be revealed as you read through the book.

The second part is called 'The Strategies'. This section contains discussions of a range of ideas that I contemplated over the summer after my graduation. They constitute a wide array of practical tips that you can apply immediately to boost your grades. The chapters are: (6) Memory Mastery, (7) Task Management, (8) Procrastination, (9) Lectures, (10) Body and Mind, (11) Study Environment, (12) Coursework and (13) Exams. I talk about my experiences dealing with each topic and how I raised my grades to a first-class level. Do note that while some of these ideas contain more of my personal experience, others also come from educational and experimental psychology, areas that can be extremely helpful.

The journey

The road to a first is tough, but apply the techniques outlined in this book and your chances of success will be greatly improved. You will learn how a belief in your abilities drives performance, how and why happy students outperform their more miserable counterparts, how to beat procrastination, how to manage your workload and much more. But even if you use all the techniques, you still have to work hard. One of my favourite quotes, from an unknown author, puts this thought quite plainly: 'All the so-called "secrets of success" will not work unless you do!' In this book I lay out the plan, but at the end of the day it is up to you to put it into practice. The ideas I share helped me attain a first-class degree and if you also implement and personalise them, your grades will rise. If a once average 2:1 student such as I was can do it, so can you!

Part 1

The Fundamentals

1

Degree Choice

Interview snippet

First-class degree student: Hannah Kelly[1]
Degree: Chemistry
Institution: Oxford University

'At 17 years old I had no idea what to do with my life so I simply picked a subject I enjoyed. Over the past four years I've had a love–hate relationship with chemistry but following my final year spent in research, I'd have to say I loved it.'

[1] This student chose not to be named, so an alias has been used.

The easy degree vs the hard degree

Numbers, and in particular statistics, can reveal much about university degrees, yet they are also incredibly easy to misinterpret. For instance, did you know that mathematical sciences have the highest percentage of students graduating with first-class degrees? In the academic year 2009/10, a whopping 30 per cent of maths students graduated with a first (HESA, 2011). Does that mean that the subject is as easy as the numbers imply? I'm sure you would agree that maths is no piece of cake, so why do so many maths students get a first?

One reason could be that in many areas of maths answers are more categorical than in other disciplines, and this makes it easier to achieve higher marks in exams and coursework. In maths, your answer can be explicitly asserted to be either right or wrong. In subjects like business studies and other social sciences, things aren't always quite as clear, so in these instances, merit is usually given to how a case is built and there is less emphasis on the one true and correct answer. Bluntly put, in maths you can get 100 per cent in an exam; in other subjects such as law, no matter how brilliant your answer is, you can never get 100 per cent.

I know at first hand how hard law is as a subject. In the law modules I studied, I know of only one student who managed to get a first in the exams. Despite cramming with what we thought were perfect answers and using as many case examples as we could, the majority of the class came out with 2:2s. It is no surprise, then, that in 2009/10 only 7 per cent of law students got a first. The statistics suggest that law is a very difficult subject.

Nevertheless, the idea that law is a lot less definitive than maths and that therefore that is why fewer law students get a first seems somewhat simplistic. It may be impossible for students to score 100 per cent in law, but this should not stop an equal number of students from scoring at least the minimum mark (usually 70 per cent) required to attain a first. I believe that something else is at play here. In this chapter I will dig a little deeper and discuss what we can learn from maths students in order to help with degree choices.

Popularity, passion and prior knowledge

Looking at university applicants for 2010, it is interesting to find that over 100,000 students applied to do a law degree, making it one of the most popular courses. Maths, on the other hand, was only slightly more popular than accounting; the degree received less than half the number of applications for law, approximately 41,000 students applying to do maths in 2010 (UCAS, 2011).

In short, then, it seems that whereas maths is quite an unpopular discipline, yet one where a huge proportion of its students graduate with first-class degrees, the opposite is true of law. A number of factors may be responsible for this phenomenon, but of all these, I suspect that two play a particularly important role in determining how well students perform. The factors are: a genuine interest in the subject area; and prior knowledge of the subject.

Lots of people want to do a law degree, but are they all as passionate about the subject itself as they are about the exorbitant graduate starting salaries – known to have peaked at £100,000 in 2000 (Verkaik, 2000)? I doubt it. Maths, on the other hand, has fewer such incentives. It requires a higher level of commitment and passion to want to do it at university level. There is less glamour to the subject and this in itself acts as a filter in applications – only students who are truly committed to the subject apply to do it. These students have a true passion for the subject, and they are prepared to put in the effort to do well.

But surely, if law students work very hard, they too can perform just as well as maths students, can't they? Not quite so. Like maths students, law undergraduates do work hard. They know that their course and career path will be no walk in the park. In fact, in one survey, 90 per cent of all students applying for law expected to work in a high-stress environment, with long working hours (Birchall, 2007). Even so, while they are prepared to work hard (and many of them do work diligently), the majority start their degree with a clear disadvantage. Remember the friend I mentioned earlier, the only one who got a first in a law module in my class? Guess what? He came to university having already done law as an A-level!

At most universities, you cannot do a maths degree without having an A-level in maths. In fact, a number of universities require students not only to do the standard A-level, but to supplement it with a more advanced version, further mathematics. These students are better prepared for their degree. Moreover, in 2011, 44.7 per cent of students taking an A-level in maths got an A grade or higher (Joint Council for Qualifications, 2011). This sets them up well for further success in higher education. In contrast, law degrees are less stringent in their requirements. In most cases, you don't need law at A-level to do it at university and many students have a range of non-related A-levels when they start their course. Although many universities argue that this is not particularly disadvantageous, there are clear differences in performance between students who have some prior knowledge of the subject and those who do not. Not surprisingly, only 18.4 per cent of students taking law at A-level got an A grade or higher. This means that even among the fraction of students who have a law A-level when they start their law degree, a smaller percentage of them got an A than those in maths.

Your choice

So you can see that a genuine interest in the subject and having prior knowledge are key to attaining a first. Therefore, in choosing a degree, you should first ensure that it is one for which you have such a passion that you are willing to expend a great amount of effort in mastering it. Many maths students show both of these characteristics: they love challenges and solving problems, and they are prepared to put in the work. They chose a maths degree because, frankly, they enjoy maths. And for this, they are more likely to be rewarded with a first than students in other subject areas.

In the case of law, we saw that things are very different. Indeed, it is rare to find a lazy lawyer – hard work is imbued in their persona – but if I may speculate for a moment, a good number of law students do not have the same level of interest in their subject as maths students, and they do not enjoy their course as much. No wonder depression is rife in law schools; it has been reported that up to 40 per cent of law students may experience depression as the result of the law school experience itself (McKinney, 2002). In a later chapter you will see that happiness affects academic performance, but for now we will simply say that, unfortunately, effort with no passion makes it harder to achieve higher grades. So what can you do?

Forging passion

So as we have seen, to be academically successful you should have some passion for your chosen subject area. This is a necessary foundation for success. If, however, you are already on a course and you find that it is rather boring and uninspiring, it is worth noting that a number of options are open to you. Two of these are top of my list (although there are many more).

First, attempt to forge some kind of zeal for the subject. Many things can be made interesting and fun if you try hard enough. For example, one of the modules I was required to complete was accounting policy. On the surface, this seemed very boring. This was until I discovered that the module was essentially about the tensions between various interest groups. All of a sudden, accounting policy turned into something more interesting: conflict resolution. Many subjects have such underlying themes and ideas that are captivating but tend to be overlooked, masked by a plethora of facts that at first sight can make the topic boring. Find these underlying themes and you will be surprised how much more interested in the subject you can become.

The second option could be considered to be among a set of last-resort strategies. And I say this because sometimes students are surprised at how much more they can enjoy a subject only after they become good at it. But if all else fails, you could look at course alternatives within your department to see if anything else interests you. I advise that you seek support, speak to your tutors and learn more about what the options are before you really consider changing course.

Prior knowledge

Maths students have an advantage at university: as already discussed, virtually all of them did maths at A-level and nearly half of them got an A or higher in it. So you may be wondering, how can you have the same edge if your A-levels are not quite so related to your degree? There is not a significant amount that you can do here, but one of the ways in which you can make a better degree choice is by basing your decision around not only your interests, but also your strengths.

Do you have a way with words or numbers? Are you a great analytical thinker? Do you love or hate coursework? These are some of the questions you can ask yourself while researching what degree you would like to do. Given time, you could also prepare for your degree over the summer by looking at some introductory textbooks. Yes, this is a very geeky thing to do, but it allows you to hit the ground running once you start your course.

Summary

The first fundamental step to academic success is to make sure that you take a suitable degree. In this chapter, we looked at how many law students work very hard but fail to achieve a first because they seem to lack a genuine interest in the subject and do not have sufficient levels of prior knowledge to be successful. Maths students, on the other hand, are in shorter supply as only those who are really passionate about the subject tend to apply for the course; that, combined with a similar work ethic to law students and, importantly, prior knowledge of their course, means that a much greater proportion of these candidates gain a first-class degree – 30 per cent compared to only 7 per cent of law graduates. In light of this, I suggest that your degree choice should take into account three factors in particular: a genuine interest in the subject, prior knowledge of the course and your individual strengths. So whether you are applying for English Literature, Art, History or Engineering, think about your motivations and consider building on your knowledge of the subject area before you enter higher education.

2

The Growth Mindset

Interview snippet

First-class student: Sabial Hanif
Degree: Economics
Institution: University of Birmingham

'I have been fortunate enough to value the importance of education from an early age. I learnt that a good education would open doors for a better future for myself. I also recognised the importance of always challenging myself to reach the potential I believed I possessed as an individual. It was this mindset that helped me attain good grades throughout my academic education.'

Beliefs make a difference

7th graders

In a New York City public school, the progress of 373 students entering the 7th grade (year 8 in the United Kingdom) was followed over a period of two years by researchers from Stanford University and Columbia University (Blackwell *et al.*, 2007). The 7th grade marks the transition from elementary school to junior high and is often challenging because the difficulty of the academic content goes up a notch – very much like the transition in the United Kingdom from GCSEs to A-levels, and from A-levels to university. In the study, students answered a questionnaire at the start of the year that assessed their goals and beliefs about intelligence and effort. Views varied widely, with two notable extremes.

Some students believed that you have a fixed level of intelligence and there is nothing you can do to change it, while others believed that you could significantly change how intelligent you are.

The researchers conducting the study then went on to track the maths test scores of the students by obtaining their grades twice a year for two years. While the quality of teaching at the school remained fairly consistent and was not – as the researchers put it – 'particularly progressive or innovative', by the end of the study the contrast in results was stark. Students who believed that they could change their level of intelligence significantly outperformed those who believed that they were born with a fixed level of intelligence.

In another study, the same researchers assessed whether a positive change in beliefs and attitudes could lead to higher levels of achievement. This time a different school was used, with a sample of relatively low-achieving students. In the experiment, two structured workshops were delivered to the students. One group was taught that intelligence was something they could develop (using analogies such as muscles becoming stronger), while the other group was merely given lessons on memory and the opportunity to discuss academic topics of interest to its members. The maths grades of the two groups were tracked over the course of the study and once again the results were clear-cut: the students who were taught that intelligence could be developed showed the greatest improvement in maths grades, while those who were not showed little change. Which group of students do you think that most first-class degree students would be in?

The stereotype threat

Do boys perform better than girls in sciences and technology-based subjects? It turns out that if you are a girl, the mere consideration of such a thought could impair your academic performance. I learnt of this peculiar notion when I came across the results of a study published in the *Journal of Experimental Social Psychology* in 1999. The researchers, Steven Spencer, Claude Steele and Diane Quinn, administered a difficult maths exam to a group of women and men from a pool of highly capable university students. (Note that maths tests are not the only way of measuring intelligence. I suspect that researchers have a preference for it as it is easy to mark answers as being right or wrong. Testing for other types of intelligence such as creativity is nowhere near so simple.) Spencer and his colleagues were sure to pick only students who had scored higher than 85 per cent of their peer group on the maths section of their university entrance exams. So while the test was tough, it was within their level of competency. Before the tests were administered, the researchers split the students into two groups. They told the students in one group that the test had shown gender differences in the past; the other group were told that no gender differences had been noticed in previous results. Guess what happened after the two groups took the maths test? The female students in the first group (those who were told that there had been gender differences in performance) did significantly worse than their male counterparts. In the second group, however, females performed at the same level as the males (Spencer et al., 1999).

It turns out that if people are made aware of a stereotype to which they could succumb, the risk of fulfilling the stereotype increases significantly. Psychologists call this the *stereotype threat*. It is part of the reason that children from poor backgrounds perform worse than those from richer backgrounds when they are told that the test they are taking measures intellectual ability (Croizet & Claire, 1998); why white men perform poorly in maths when they are told that their results will be compared to Asian men (who are stereotypically thought to excel at maths; Aronson et al., 1999); and why black students underperform their white counterparts when, before a test, they are asked to state their race, or when they are told that the test is a measure of intelligence (Aronson et al., 2002).

While such findings are difficult to explain fully, psychologists argue that the stereotype threat operates by diverting brain resources away from the task at hand in order to combat feelings of doubt. And even if you do not believe a certain stereotype, once you are aware of it, trying your hardest not to fulfil it can significantly impair your performance (Forbes et al., 2008). Fortunately, learning about the stereotype effect can get us closer to finding ways of combating it.

Growing intelligence

The question of whether intelligence is shaped by nature or nurture is still hotly debated and in my research I could not find a definitive answer. However, if there is anything we can learn from studies such as those I shared earlier, it is that there is an aspect of intelligence that is flexible. Of course, some people are naturally very smart, but convince them that intelligence is fixed, or draw their attention to a stereotype (for instance, make them believe a fake statistic that tall people are rubbish at economics), and you will find that their performance on tests that supposedly measure 'intelligence' is impaired. Judged by performances on such tests, a naturally smart person could be thought to be less intelligent than they actually are. So the message is that intelligence is not purely fixed.

Now, I am not saying that everyone can increase their intelligence by an infinite amount and get a first-class degree. What I am saying is that by changing certain beliefs and thoughts, it is possible to expand your intelligence, though obviously there are limits. Nevertheless, this book is not about limits. It is about pushing yourself to an achievable level of success. To help you with this aspiration, here are two key lessons that you can take away from this discussion to help you achieve higher grades.

Lessons about beliefs

The first lesson is that if you believe that intelligence is fixed, you are likely to perform worse than if you do not. In the first set of studies described above, it was the students who believed that intelligence is malleable who worked harder to get better. These were also the students who did not give up easily. They had what Carol Dweck (one of the key researchers in the area) calls the *growth mindset* (Dweck, 2006). On the other hand, students who believed that intelligence is fixed gave up more easily on challenging tasks and attributed their poor performance to an innate lack of intelligence. These students had what Dweck calls a *fixed mindset*.

University students can be categorised in a similar way. In fact, at university I found it easy to identify students who had a fixed mindset – I was one of them. A classmate would perform extremely well in an exam or achieve an outstanding grade for a piece of coursework and many of us would give all the credit to a mysterious and ambiguous notion: talent. No credit was ever given to the hard work the student and others had actually put in and the conclusion was that these students were simply naturally intelligent. However, the more I started to hang around high-performing students, the more I discovered how hard they really worked. Admittedly, natural aptitude does exist, but I will say it again: the right beliefs and hard work can also get you a long way.

Consider Will Smith (to whom we shall return in the next chapter). He is not the most traditionally talented actor, yet in 2007, *Newsweek* crowned him the most powerful actor on the planet. As a rapper, he is not the greatest lyricist either, yet in 1989 he took home the first Grammy to be given to a rap artist. Guess what type of mindset Will Smith's life philosophy is based on? Here's a clue. It is based on four simple words: "I can do it" (Grant, 2006).

The second lesson is that if you adjust your beliefs and your attitude towards intelligence, ability and talent, your performance will also change. Adopting a growth mindset is what, in one study, led to black students outperforming their counterparts who had a fixed mindset (Aronson *et al.*, 2002). In another study, female students taking a test garnered increased self-esteem after being told that the female invigilator administering the exam had also designed it. The mere presence of such a role model led them to perform better than female students who had a male invigilator (Marx & Roman, 2002). Such findings are reassuring because they show that no matter what your gender, race or socioeconomic background is, altering your beliefs and having a growth mindset can have an impact on how well you do.

Maintaining a growth mindset

Once you have developed the right mindset, you need to take steps to maintain it. There were times when I would lose confidence in my ability to achieve a first. Times when I would sit through two hours of a lecture and not understand a single concept the lecturer was talking about.

Times when I would look at a question from a past paper and not have a clue how to answer it. And times when I would spend many hours on an essay, only to receive a 2:2 level of mark. Indeed, on many occasions I pondered whether it was better for me simply to settle for a 2:1 degree and expend less effort. Thank goodness I never settled!

When you end up in this situation – and believe me, at some point you will – you can use it to your advantage. The way I saw it, whenever doubt arose, it was a calling to do some extra work. So, for example, when you go to a lecture and you come out not having understood a single concept, it is not because you are less intelligent than your classmates; indeed, you may find, as I did, that your classmates were similarly dumbfounded. The key is not to let such doubts destroy your belief in your ability to attain a first. Rather, see this doubt as a great awakening that you need to fill a gap in your knowledge. Some additional reading and practice at exercise questions, for example, could be all that you require. By reworking doubts in this way, you won't panic. Instead, you will maintain a growth mindset and will be motivated to take action to improve.

Summary

Motivational talk – like 'If you believe you can do it, you will do it!' – sometimes sounds corny and unrealistic. But in this chapter I have discussed research demonstrating that varying beliefs and mindsets can indeed lead to varying results in performance. In particular, having a growth mindset can lead to you working harder and bypassing hindrances such as the stereotype threat. This is why the second fundamental step to take towards getting a first-class degree is having a growth mindset. Yes, there are some students who have a natural aptitude for a subject – and maybe you are one of them, maybe you are not – but this doesn't matter as much in a world where, if you apply yourself, you can stretch your abilities to new heights. You may not believe that you can get a first right now, but you should at least believe that you can get it given time and effort. Have a growth mindset and you will be on your way to growing into a first-class student.

3

Work Ethic

Interview snippet

First-class student: Kimberley Hill
Degree: Economics
Institution: University of Nottingham

'It was always at the back of my mind – that I would love to get a first. But in the first year I got quite a lot of 2:1s and thought maybe that was what my intelligence equated to at university. In the first term of the second year, things got worse and I didn't do too well in my exams (I averaged 58.5 per cent). I thought my dreams of a first were all but gone. However, I really got my head down in the second semester and managed to pull my average up to 65.5 per cent. By the first semester of the third year, I had pulled my average up to 70 per cent!'

Will power

At the age of 16, Willard Christopher 'Will' Smith experienced a defining moment in his life: his first girlfriend cheated on him. In the grand scheme of things this may sound trivial, but the impact it had on Will was not. In his mind, he believed that his girlfriend cheated on him because he was not good enough. This saddening event led him to make a conscious decision: that he would never be not good enough again. He would strive to work as hard as it took to be the very best he could be.

Will Smith began to live his life with a new attitude. For instance, though he had no intention of going to university, his academic efforts in high school meant that his grades were high enough to present him with the opportunity to attend the Massachusetts Institute of Technology, the world's number one engineering university. It helps, of course, that his mother, an alumna of Carnegie Mellon (another prestigious university), instilled in him the belief that education was invaluable and so deserved unwavering effort. You could say that the stage was set for Will to excel academically, but he had other plans. Regardless, he was still remarkably more determined than the average teenager and was wholeheartedly committed to being more than just 'good enough'.

Will Smith's father, Willard Christopher Smith, Sr., also had a notable influence on his work ethic. After serving in the US Air Force, Will Smith Sr. took the entrepreneurial path and started a refrigerator business in which he worked diligently for seven days a week. His determination and discipline clearly rubbed off on the young Will. The following account is an exemplar of the kind of lessons Will learnt from his father.

In an interview with the magazine *Reader's Digest*, Will remembered a time when his father decided to renovate his shop by tearing down an old wall that towered 16 feet high and ran 40 feet long. Will, then 12 years old, and his younger brother were set to work on it over the summer with their father. To the boys the job seemed daunting and unfeasible. As Will said, 'We were standing there thinking there will never, ever, be a wall here again.' Laying brick by brick, it would take them all summer, winter and spring to finish the new wall. But when it was done on time, their father told them, 'Now, don't you ever tell me there's something you can't do.' Will learnt an important lesson. In his words, 'The thing I connect to is: I do not have to build a perfect wall today. I just have to lay a perfect brick. Just lay one brick, dude.' These experiences were the foundations of what Will now calls a 'sickening' work ethic.

Will Smith's work ethic

Surprisingly, Will Smith has always considered himself to be of average natural talent, despite being once crowned the most powerful actor on the planet (Smith, 2007). In particular, a career box office of $4.4 billion put his success above that of Johnny Depp and Ben Stiller (arguably more talented actors), who both trailed behind in box office sales. You may wonder how a person who claims to be of average natural talent got to such a position. The answer is clear: his work ethic. When asked in a CBS interview why he thought he had been so successful, Will Smith answered:

> I've never really viewed myself as particularly talented. Where I excel is [in my] ridiculous, sickening work ethic. You know, while the other guy is sleeping, I'm working. While the other guy is eating, I'm working. While the other guy is making love, I mean, I'm making love too, but I'm working really hard at it! (CBS News, 2008)

Simply put, Will Smith is one of the hardest-working people in show business and he really does believe that he can achieve anything he puts his mind to. He has a growth mindset. This is the reason he works so hard. It is the reason why in the run-up to filming *Ali*, he consistently trained for six hours a day, five days a week, in order to put on 30 pounds of muscle (O'Donnell, 2002). It is also why he can be serious in saying, 'People laugh, but I swear to you right now, sittin' here: I believe if I set my mind to it, within the next 15 years I would be president of the United States' (Sager, 1998). In essence, Will Smith's work ethic is about working the hardest you can to achieve your utmost potential. This is an extremely admirable trait, which if we mere mortals were to imitate would no doubt lead us to significant successes of our own. But what precisely can we learn from such a star to inspire us to do better?

Lessons from the stars

Looking at Will Smith and a number of other immensely successful people, it is possible to identify a number of things that spur them on to do well. If we could break up their work ethic and boil it down to a number of useful ideas that students can adopt, I would say that they are (1) find your leverage; (2) be patient and take one step at a time; and (3) put your head down and run hard. I discuss each of these in turn below.

Find your leverage

Some of Will Smith's leverage came from his girlfriend cheating on him. He believed that she cheated because he was not good enough. But instead of sulking, the incident inspired him to become the best person he could be. His parents also provided additional leverage. A firm mother who believed in education inspired him to become a life-long learner and an avid reader, while his father ingrained in him the principles of discipline, resilience and determination.

Other stars have recounted similar turning points in their lives. J. K. Rowling, the first female billionaire novelist (*Guinness World Records*, 2011), once considered herself the biggest failure she had ever known. Seven years after graduating, she had a failed marriage, lacked a job and was extremely poor. However, many years later at a commencement speech at Harvard University, she pointed out that had she not hit rock bottom she would never have found the determination to focus on the one area in life where she felt she truly belonged, writing (Rowling, 2008). From such accounts, we can see that a strong work ethic can arise from events or circumstances that inspire you to put in 100 per cent effort. *This* is leverage – something that will get you to change gear and work harder.

However, leverage does not have to emerge from miserable events. Finding an already successful role model could be your leverage. Do you remember the discussion of the stereotype effect in Chapter 2, and how its effects were wiped out by the presence of a suitable role model? The female students in the study, for example, ended up performing better at an exam when the invigilator was female and purported to be the person who designed the test. In essence, this invigilator acted as a role model to the female students. It could be said that she was their leverage.

You can also attain your leverage in this manner. Great role models to look to for inspiration could be hard-working parents, siblings or friends who have already graduated. And if this isn't enough leverage, you could think about the large amount of money you are spending to go to university. Why not attempt to get the highest possible return on your investment? Getting a first-class degree would put you in the top 14 per cent of the student population and this opens up career opportunities that may not be available otherwise. Another form of leverage I often hear from students who got a first was that they saw university as a once-in-a-lifetime opportunity and they wanted to graduate knowing that they had done their very best. To all intents and purposes their leverage was to avoid regret: the regret of looking back and wondering what grades they would have received had they worked just a little harder. This could be your leverage too.

Be patient and take one step at a time

If you are currently on a 2:1 or maybe even a 2:2, it is unlikely that you will become a first-class student overnight. What you must understand is that the change will take both time and consistent but manageable effort. People like J. K. Rowling, though successful in other fields, serve as great inspiration when it comes to patience and persistence. Did you know that she started writing stories at the age of around 5 or 6, and that it took over 20 years before her first book, *Harry Potter and the Philosopher's Stone*, hit the shelves (*The Scotsman*, 2003)?

Achieving a first is less of a grand feat and in my case, it took me three years – I averaged 2:1s in my first and second years. In fact, as mentioned in the introduction, my first piece of written coursework received 55 per cent! It was a disappointment, but I was not entirely disheartened. I knew that there was work to be done and that I had three years to get to my target. So be patient with your progress, because growth takes a while. Start early, stay patient and work hard!

Put your head down and run hard

It is natural to feel competitive at university. You sit an exam or submit a piece of coursework, and when the results are out, the comparisons with peers begin. You check to see if you outperformed your friends, or whether they did better than you. If it is the latter, and you worked really hard, you lose confidence in yourself and think that perhaps your friend who whipped up the essay in one night is simply smarter. Try your best to avoid these comparisons. Such a mentality is a major reason why, for example, income levels have risen in the West while happiness levels have not followed suit (Layard *et al.*, 2009). When people keep comparing themselves to other people, even though they are better off than they were in the past, they are never satisfied. It is much better to put your head down and make sure that the only person you are competing with is yourself. I advise that you try as much as you can to compare your achievements to your past performance, not to that of your peers.

When I started to write my dissertation, I did not set out to beat everyone and have the highest mark in the class. That was not my goal. Instead, I decided that I was going to work at my own absolute best. I was going to push myself to produce the very best piece of work I could and no matter what result I got, I would not have the regret of not trying hard enough. To avoid such remorse, I put an enormous amount of effort into writing my dissertation and to my surprise I won the prize for the highest dissertation mark. You will truly be surprised at what you can achieve if you focus on your own growth. Even Will Smith is astonished at how he got to where he is today. When asked whether his success surprised him, he once answered:

> For a long time now, I have been beyond anything that I ever dreamed. I just put my head down and run hard, and I am almost always surprised when I look up and see where I am. (Grant, 2006)

Summary

Many successful students clearly adopt a work ethic that goes beyond what is required merely to pass a course. I remember going to a computing lab at Imperial College London and seeing students who would stay until the late hours of the night to perfect their software. There is no escaping hard work if you want to do your best. Thankfully, having a bit of leverage can push you on to achieve more. In this chapter, I have shared with you some ways of attaining such leverage and how you could then couple it with patience and a focus on personal growth to do better at university. These ideas are what form the third fundamental step to academic success, a work ethic – the ability to put in more effort than the average student.

4

Happiness and Grades

Interview snippet

First-class student: Catherine Allen
Degree: Theatre and Performance Studies
Institution: University of Warwick

'Most of the time I was happy at university and quite fulfilled. Getting a good mark in an essay obviously gives you a boost, but I also found that a close network of friends is very important to being happy. The times I felt most down were when I'd been working really hard on an essay, or on my films, and working so much that I hadn't had time to spend with my friends.'

Okinawans, university students, friends and loners

To the south of Japan, about 900 miles from Tokyo, lies Okinawa, a prefecture that consists of over 100 miniature islands. There is something unique about this place. Aside from being the birthplace of karate, Okinawa has the longest disability-free life expectancy in the world (Buettner, 2009) and, when compared to America, it has five times as many people living to, and beyond, 100 years of age (Okinawa Centenarian Study, n.d.). The people of Okinawa age much better than anyone else on the planet, but what is the key to their longevity? The answers are to be found in the Okinawa Centenarian Study, which has now been running for over a quarter of a century and has identified a number of contributing factors to longevity. Along with a healthy diet, exercise and spirituality, a contributing factor to the youthfulness of Okinawans was identified in the social networks they cultivate. The study found that the Okinawans' positive social ties are a significant source of happiness and psychological well-being that adds many years to their lives (Willcox et al., 2001).

But perhaps you are not concerned about making it to 100 years of age. And to be frank, as a university student I was more concerned about getting my next student loan instalment than worrying about ageing. Nevertheless, what we can take from the above findings is that friends are pretty important for psychological and physiological well-being. In particular, having a good set of friends and a decent social life has been found to be a good predictor of how happy people are. For example, a study by two prominent psychologists, Ed Diener and Martin Seligman, involved the intensive study of 222 university students at the University of Illinois. It found that the top 10 per cent of consistently happy students were all highly social and had stronger social relationships than the very unhappy students. Furthermore, the very happy group spent the least time alone and the most amount of time socialising (Diener & Seligman, 2002). Of course, this shouldn't be a surprise because we all know that being a loner is no fun, but surprisingly, researchers have found that excessive solitude could ultimately take years off your life – more than could obesity or a lack of exercise (Holt-Lunstad et al., 2010).

There are many factors – some within our control, others not – that can contribute to happiness, but the focus in this chapter will be on what students usually have the most control over: our social lives. Things like money and material wealth certainly play a role, but if the Okinawans and the sample of university students in Diener and Seligman's study are anything to go by, you can build great conditions for increased happiness by simply improving your social life. And if doing so has been estimated by socioeconomists to be worth up to an additional £85,000 a year in terms of life satisfaction (Powdthavee, 2008), it must be worth some consideration. However, before we delve into how you can nurture the conditions for being happier, let's explore what happiness has to do with academic performance.

Happiness and academic performance

If you are miserable at university, do you think that your academic performance will be affected? Even if you are experiencing personal problems and choose to use academic work as a distraction and an escape, do you really think that you will perform as well as if you are enjoying your time at university? The answer, more often than not, is that the more miserable you are, the worse you perform. Although some studies suggest that people primed to be in a negative mood do better at some analytical tasks (Schwarz, 2002), and that in some cases being happy or sad appears to make no difference (Nadler *et al.*, 2010), an ever-growing body of research shows that people in a good mood perform better at numerous cognitive activities.

Nevertheless, do happy students really get better grades? In a longitudinal study that tracked the progress of 5th graders (year 6 in the United Kingdom), researchers Angela Duckworth and Patrick Quinn found that well-being (or happiness) did in fact predict academic performance. While such studies often have causality uncertainties – that is, if there is a correlation between x and y, does x cause y, or does y cause x? Or is there some other factor, z, that causes x? – this particular study discovered a form of reciprocal causality. The students in the study who reported higher well-being were discovered to be more likely to earn higher grades despite their IQ, age or previous academic performance. In addition, performing well academically tended to make the students happier (Duckworth & Quinn, 2007). In essence, if you are happy you are likely to perform better, and if you perform better you are likely to be happier.

The reasons such differences in performance emerge are not yet entirely clear, but psychologists have uncovered a number of explanations, some of which will be considered in this chapter.

Stronger immune system

Positive emotions have been found to affect both the mind and the body in many complex ways. For example, did you know that people with higher positive emotions have a stronger immune system? In one study, which as a penniless student I would have gladly taken part in, over 300 volunteers were paid quite a lot of money to be infected with a common cold virus. Their conditions and environment were then carefully monitored and controlled over the days that followed. By the end of the study, Carnegie Mellon professor Dr Cohen and his team discovered that people who were happier were not only less likely to catch a cold, they also had less severe symptoms (Cohen *et al.*, 2003). Putting these results into the context of academic performance, it is possible that happier students are less likely to have sick days. This means that more quality time can be spent attending lectures, revising and preparing for exams.

Increased creativity

Happiness also affects how the brain works. For instance, one series of experiments found that when university students were shown a range of video clips to bring about feelings of amusement, contentment, neutrality, anger or anxiety, their responses to subsequent mental activities varied. Students who watched penguins play around, and were generally amused by it, tended to have a wider scope of attention. That is, they were more likely to see the bigger picture in the assigned visual task. Furthermore, these students had a broader range of answers when asked to list all the things they would have liked to do at that time (Fredrickson & Branigan, 2005).

Positive emotions have the ability to broaden our thinking and, not surprisingly, a number of other studies (Daubman *et al.*, 1987) have linked happiness to increased creativity. When you are in a good mood, you have an increased tendency to connect ideas in new and interesting ways. For students, this can be an effective way of learning new material (we shall see in Chapter 6 how linking various disparate ideas can boost memory, for example). It also means that if you are a generally positive person, you are more likely to have more creative and insightful answers to questions in coursework and exams. And this is what often separates first-class answers from the average.

More resilience and optimism

Happiness doesn't stop there. One more example of how the mind can be affected by mood comes from a series of experiments that were carried out by researchers at the University of Virginia. They found that when it came to estimating how steep a hill was, people who were put in a good mood by listening to music in a major key − 'happy music' − judged it to be less steep than those who were put in a depressed mood by listening to minor-key music − 'sad music'. How big was the difference in perception? People who listened to sad music thought that the hill was 150 per cent steeper when compared to the estimates of those who listened to happy music (Riener *et al.*, 2011).

Such experiments are, of course, simplistic, but this one in particular is a good reminder of how being happy can lead us to being more optimistic about our chances of success. While happy people tend to be more confident and more willing to give things a go, sad people tend to make 'mountains out of molehills' (Clore & Palmer, 2009). And this isn't necessarily a bad thing, because it can sober you up to be better prepared. But if you see mountains instead of molehills too often, and are discouraged from attempting achievable things (like getting a first), then perhaps you need a little more happiness to help you see things in a more optimistic light.

Next, we shall look at how you can cultivate happiness by one of the most accessible methods to students: having an active social life.

Active social life

In the first and second terms of my final year, I went out almost every Saturday night and rarely ever said no to social events. While I was not exactly a party animal, like a few of my friends were, I hardly missed out on the fun aspect of being a student. I always met and made new friends each term and maintained strong social ties both on and off campus. Since human beings are social animals by nature, you should ensure that you at least have a healthy and active social life at university. As discussed earlier, this can lead not only to increased happiness but also a boost in your academic performance. Here are a number of simple ways in which you can enhance your social life:

Join societies

Societies provide the easiest way of making new friends and finding activities to do with other students. In your first year you can join as many as you like, though as you progress to later years you might want to cut down on your commitments. Also, feel free to switch between societies from time to time. In my first year I joined the breakdance society. In the second, I joined the university radio station. In my final year, I co-founded and ran the entrepreneurs' society in which I acted as vice-president. Being involved in all these societies meant that not only was I making new friends, I also had a good number of social activities to take part in, which made university so much more fun.

Don't forget friends from home

Keep in touch with friends from home. If you are an international student this may be difficult, as you cannot take a flight home every weekend, but even then, when you make trips back for Christmas and Easter, you will find ample time to catch up with friends who have known you for much longer than people at university. It is important to keep these connections, because you may find that in the first few months you do not have any friends who are close enough to confide in if times get tough.

Have more happy friends

When you go out to socialise, try to mix with positive people. Happiness is contagious, but so is unhappiness. This is not to say that you should abandon your friends as soon as they hit a bout of depression, just that you should be somewhat selective about whom you mix with. A telling study by Nicholas Christakis, a physician from Harvard University, and James Fowler, a sociologist from the University of California, found that for each additional happy friend you have, you increase your probability of being happy by about 9 per cent (Fowler & Christakis, 2008a). To put this figure into perspective, increasing your income by £6,000 increases your probability of being happy by only 2 per cent or so (Fowler & Christakis, 2008b). Therefore, socialise and mix with more happy people if you can and their happiness will rub off on you.

Say yes to more

Even if you don't feel like it, whenever a friend invites you out, try to say yes unless you really have to stay in. Simply not feeling like it is usually a poor excuse for missing out on the fun aspects of being at university. And you don't have to be an extrovert to enjoy the company of others. Happiness research shows that introverts can experience a boost of as much as 60 per cent in the average intensity of positive feelings when with others compared to when alone (Diener & Biswas-Diener, 2008: 52). My take is this: you are only a student once and it is often the best and easiest time of your life to socialise, so make the most of it. Along the way, you will also enhance your social skills, which can be quite advantageous when it comes to employability. All in all, always remember that if you are in a bit of a depression, further isolation is only likely to make things worse, so say yes and go out!

Summary

As the English poet and writer John Masefield once said, 'the days that make us happy make us wise'. As it turns out, your academic performance has everything to do with your happiness. If you ignore your psychological well-being, your grades are likely to take a nosedive; as a result of poor grades, you could end up even more miserable. (Unless, of course, you don't care what grades you get.) ▷

Nevertheless, as we saw in this chapter, being a little happier can indeed help turn things around.

While many books and academic papers have been written on the subject of happiness, offering numerous ideas for how people can be happier, a recurrent theme in the research is social ties, of which students can readily take advantage. So whether a relationship has gone sour, your student loan has run dry or you simply feel homesick, having good friends and taking part in social activities can help lift you out of low spirits. Have an active social life and you will be in a much better position to fight off bouts of unhappiness, which could hinder your academic performance.

5

Support Systems

Interview snippet

First-class student: Ibrahim Tolulope
Degree: Accounting and Finance
Institutions: University of Birmingham and London School of Economics

'I wasn't always a straight A student. I only started to get into the habit of hard work when I got into college. This is because the majority of the friends I spent time with were hard workers. This is what motivated me.'

Bowling alone

In a telling essay (Putnam, 1995) and book (Putnam, 2001), Harvard University social scientist Robert Putnam raised awareness of an emerging trend. After digging through nearly half a million interviews collected over the previous quarter of a century, Putnam discovered that Americans were becoming increasingly more detached from family, friends and neighbours. The 1995 essay, aptly titled 'Bowling alone', summed up the substantive evidence of disengagement by the following notion: more Americans go bowling today, but bowling in organised leagues has plummeted. Putnam argued that more and more people are going through life solo and losing out on opportunities to build *social capital* – the connections between individuals that, much like physical capital such as machinery, can enhance individual productivity.

Putnam suggests that the decline in social capital may be applicable to many other contemporary societies besides America and it is a trend that presents a number of dangers. First, lower social capital adversely affects health and happiness (remember, happiness also affects academic grades). This may happen in a number of ways, but one is that a lack of social capital makes weathering crises more difficult. For example, the sociologist Glen Elder found that people who had high levels of social integration coped better in troubling times. That is, they emerged stronger and mentally healthier after major events such as the Great Depression and the Second World War (Elder, 1974, 1998; Haidt, 2006).

Another danger is that weak social connections make it more difficult to direct our behaviour towards beneficial and accepted norms. Putnam points out that people are more likely give in to their worst impulses if they don't have sufficient social capital. If that isn't bad enough, he also suggests that poor social capital hinders the flow of information that facilitates the achievement of our goals. This, in turn, thwarts effective economic production and education.

You may ask, 'What exactly do these social capital deficiency ills have to do with academic success?' As has been the pattern in previous chapters, we shall consider the answer to this question shortly.

Social capital as a support system

The effects of the presence or the lack of social capital are noticeable in students' lives in a number of ways. For example, the university experience can present the most challenging of times for freshers. Higher education institutions know this and so through a number of devices attempt to make things easier for students. Freshers' week is supposed to facilitate the immediate formation of social capital through numerous social events. You are forced to create new bonds quickly, but thankfully this is easy because everyone is in the same boat. With your new friends, you somehow manage to pull through what would normally be a terrifying and intimidating experience. Essentially, the university does its best to help you build social capital (friends in the same boat) such that you can weather a difficult time (starting university). The road to a first should be no different. You need to build a support system in the form of social capital to weather the tough times ahead. Only then will you come out of university a stronger and mentally healthier person.

The second way in which social capital affects students comes in the form of behavioural cues. We often direct our behaviour according to what our peers do. If all your friends are going out, you also feel inclined to go out. You could call this a mild form of peer pressure. It is always easier to say yes to an invitation if all your friends are going to the same event, regardless of whether you have lectures at 9 the next morning or not. Conversely, if all your friends are in the library studying, you will feel more inclined to be there too. As such, the social capital we build and the social ties we cultivate at university do have the power to affect our behaviour, both negatively and positively. Therefore, it is important to build ties that will be conducive to your academic success.

Finally, university is all about education and the flow of information. As Robert Putnam pointed out, low social capital can thwart the speed at which information flows and this cripples education. At university, if you build your social capital in a way that is conducive to your academic success (this will be detailed shortly), you will find that incomprehensible and excruciatingly difficult course material can at times be decoded by a group of friends (study buddies) who have similar goals, more quickly than when singular and individual efforts are employed.

Now that we know how social capital affects student life, let us look at how you can build yours to your benefit.

Building your social capital

At university, I had a good support system in the form of a healthy level of social capital. As discussed earlier, social capital can help you:

- Weather demanding situations more effectively.
- Maintain behaviours that are conducive to your academic success.
- Understand academic material faster via collective problem solving.

While I had no conceptual idea about what I was doing at university (in terms of social capital), looking back on it I believe that three key components acted as a support system and contributed to my social capital and academic success. These were study buddies, friends and family. Below, we look at each of these components in turn.

Study buddies

Study buddies can be a very effective support system when it comes to academic pursuits. I had a core group of friends I would go to the library with on a regular basis; not necessarily to work in a group (we only did this once or twice a month for a few hours to discuss some topics), but to know that we were not studying alone. Such friends can help you weather the academic demands of your degree. You will be in the same boat, face the same struggles and thus support each other.

With study buddies, I was often motivated to work harder. In situations where I was not working hard enough, they would slate me for slacking off. For example, in the final term of my final year, there were days when I would get up to leave the library early, only to sit back down again quickly after a friend mocked me: 'You've only been here six hours and you're leaving already? You're getting lazy, Mike!' Such study buddies, provided they are just as hard working (I advise you to find students who are smarter and more hard working than you), will also help you maintain behaviours (such as discipline) that are conducive to your academic success.

While I was never the smartest among the study buddies, we all had our unique strengths and weaknesses. As a group, we could make sense of course material much faster than if we were to go at it alone. This is not to say that whenever I did not understand something I would go off running to a study buddy who did. Rather, within the group we had an unspoken code: time permitting, you would exhaust all other means before you asked a friend for help. In this way, we respected each other's time, but were also always ready to give a helping hand.

Friends and family

Study buddies provide many forms of support. However, you should not forget that your regular friends – and, more importantly, family – can also act as a vital component in your support system. Whenever the academic work got too stressful, I always had friends I could go on nights out with. Though my study buddies were rarely keen on the typical student nights, my social circle was diverse enough that every week there was a group I could join for a night out. Have study buddies, but also diversify your social circle and have friends you can turn to for things other than studying.

In addition to friends, my family was extremely supportive. I cannot emphasise enough how much this support helped me through university. From times when I would run out of money to simply having a chat with my parents about my progress, having the family there provided a means of support that not even study buddies or university friends could have matched. Keep in touch with your family and you will be able to receive the support you so often need, moral or otherwise.

Summary

The fifth fundamental for academic success is to have some kind of support system while at university. In this chapter we saw how three components of such a system (friends, family and study buddies) will help you weather the challenges of student life and maintain behaviour that is conducive to your academic success. In particular, study buddies will also help you grasp academic content at a much faster rate than if you were to approach all of your studies alone. Also note that a support system does not have to be limited to the three components discussed. You may find, for instance, that a friendly personal tutor helps you as you progress through university. Or you may be able to take advantage of the free counseling and guidance services available at most universities. In short, build and maintain a support system and the road to a first will be less difficult.

Student to Student to Student

Part 2

The Strategies

6

Memory Mastery

Interview snippet

First-class student: **Mark Burton**
Degree: **Mathematics**
Institution: **University of Manchester**

'Try various techniques. The key to actually memorising things is unaided repetition (i.e. you can remember everything every time without any prompting). Also, I always listen to music. In my mind I figured that if I can remember/work while distracted by music, I will be able to do it in the exam without it, where my attention will be fully engaged to the task. Another tip is to compare past exams to find similarities such that you prepare for the actual exam format.'

Memory masters

Boncompagno da Signa, a twelfth-century Bolognese professor at the University of Bologna (the same city where bolognese pasta sauce originated), was very much admired by students for what appeared to be an exceptional feat of memory. Within 30 days, he could memorise the full names of 500 students as well as where they came from (Carruthers, 2008: 139). This might sound incredible, but moving further back in time we find even more dazzling memory feats. For example, Metrodorus of Scepsis – a first-century Greek writer who is thought to have been a key figure in the development of memory techniques – could memorise full conversations and repeat them back to people word for word (O'Brien, 1993). As it happens, when paper as we know it today was non-existent, it was not unusual to find orators, poets, lawyers and politicians among the early Greeks and Romans who could commit to memory speeches, legislation, whole books and other literary works, reciting them at will with 100 per cent accuracy.

More examples of memory masters are to be found in recent times. A particularly interesting story concerns the discovery of a young Russian memory master called Shereshevsky (known as S in academic circles; Luria & Bruner, 1987). At the age of 29 he worked as a journalist and in an editorial meeting, while his peers tentatively made notes and the editor handed out vast amounts of information, S wrote nothing. All he did was listen. The editor, having noticed this peculiar behaviour a number of times before, decided to confront him. By the end of the confrontation both the editor and S were amazed, though for different reasons. S was surprised at being told off and was astonished that other people had to make notes at all. The editor, on the other hand, was shocked to see that without any notes, S could reproduce the entire contents of the meeting, word for word, with perfect accuracy! Imagine if you, too, had such a memory, or perhaps even just a fraction of it, just so that you could ace some exams. In this chapter, we will explore how you can tap into some of this potential.

From average to exceptional

Do you believe that feats of memory can only be achieved by naturally gifted people, or those whose brains are perhaps structured differently? If so, then please read Chapter 2 again to remind yourself how such a belief can prevent you from fulfilling your potential. In fact, there is virtually no limit to how much information the brain can keep in its long-term memory. Once information is there, it is stored permanently. We can all have an exceptional memory provided that we practise sound memory principles and attain experience in the art of memorising (techniques that will soon be explained). If you don't believe that you can improve your memory, maybe you will be more convinced by two psychologists who went about proving just that in the 1980s.

In 1982, K. Anders Ericsson, a world-leading researcher on expertise, along with his colleague, William Chase, demonstrated that an undergraduate of average intelligence could be trained to have exceptional memory skills that closely matched those of memory masters (Ericsson & Chase, 1982). In this study an undergraduate, whose code name was SF, trained for more than 230 hours in a digit-span task over the course of 20 months. This task tests a candidate's ability to remember a set of numbers. A sequence of random digits is read to the candidate at a rate of one digit per second; if he or she remembers the full sequence correctly, an extra digit is added in the next sequence. This is repeated until a limit is reached, and this is termed the digit span.

SF started out with a digit span of seven (the level that an average person can attain). This meant that you could read him seven digits at a speed of one digit per second, and he could remember all of them. Without any sort of coaching, a very motivated SF proceeded to experiment with various methods in a self-taught manner, hoping to find a way of remembering more numbers. Initially, he tried the rehearsal method. This involves merely repeating the sequence in your head until it sticks (similar to how most students cram material). However, this could only take him as far as remembering a sequence of nine digits. It wasn't until he began to use associations (which will be explained later) that his performance at the digit-span task sky-rocketed. At his peak, he was able to attain a digit span of 82! This study demonstrates that through experience and practice, average students could indeed improve their memory practically to that of a genius. If SF could achieve such a feat, so can you. In the next section we will consider a number of techniques that you can employ in order to boost your memory.

Lessons from memory masters

Tony Buzan, a world-leading expert on the brain and learning, suggests that the keys to a perfect memory are imagination and association

(Buzan, 2006). All the examples of memory masters you have read in this chapter (including the undergraduate student who trained his memory to such brilliance) used some form of association and vivid imagination. Buzan's book *Use Your Memory* details a number of techniques and methods of association and imagination. By using some of them, I managed to improve my memory and tackled exams with increased confidence. Although the actual memory techniques given in Buzan's book go beyond the scope of this chapter, we shall look at some of the underlying principles that when used even in the most basic form, can boost your memory to a remarkable extent.

Association

The first of these principles is association. When we take in new information, we remember it more easily if it is related to something we already know. For example, if I were to ask you to remember the digits 314365999, it might take you a bit longer to commit them to memory if you simply used the rehearsal method; that is, repeating the sequence in your head until it sticks. On the other hand, notice the following: 314 is similar to Π (pie – 3.14); 365 is the number of days in a year; and 999 is the telephone number for the police in Britain. You could even convert the sequence into a sentence: 'A *pie* a *year* for the *police*.' Such an exercise has the ability to make a stronger impression on your long-term memory. That is the power of association.

Imagination

The second principle is imagination. We find it easier to remember the peculiar and the out of the ordinary. Why? Because they vividly capture our imagination. If you came across a dancing pink elephant, you would never forget it because you have never come across a dancing pink elephant before. Our brains simply have a much easier time remembering things that stimulate our senses and evoke emotion. For instance, in a law module on my course, practically all the students remembered the case of *Donoghue v Stevenson [1932]*. This is because it involved a customer who fell ill after drinking ginger beer from a bottle that contained the remains of a dead snail! In a nutshell, the more our imagination is aroused, the more we remember.

Association + imagination

The examples given above were chosen for convenience to illustrate a point. In reality, the information you will have to remember for your exams will not associate so easily with anything you already know. Nor will it capture your imagination so effortlessly. As such, when you begin to learn new material or want to revise, always make a conscious effort to create vivid and imaginative associations with what you already know. It may take work, but it will commit the information to your long-term memory more effectively. Consider the following example, taken from my finance module at university.

In a *bear market*, the stock market experiences a downturn and investors generally have lower confidence. They are also more pessimistic and fearful. In a *bull market*, investors have more confidence and an anticipation of future price increases pulls the stock market up. If you were new to finance, how would you remember which effect (upturn or downturn) goes with the bull or bear market? A quick way to remember this new knowledge would be to use association and imagination. Our lecturer suggested the following. In bullfighting, when a bull attempts to attack a matador, using its horns it lunges in an upward direction, hoping to send the poor bullfighter off into the air – that is, a stock market upturn. A bear, on the other hand, will attack its aggressors by downward thrusts of its fists and claws, attacking in a downward manner – that is, a stock market downturn. Therefore, a bull market is associated with a bull attacking upwards (stock prices rise), while a bear market is associated with a bear attacking downwards (stock prices fall).

Isn't that an easier method of remembering than learning by the repetition of definitions until they stick? At first sight, the association method may seem long-winded, but I can assure you that learning in this manner means that the information is ingrained into your long-term memory; you are then less likely to forget it.

Sometimes the information from your course will have associations you can expand on to make things more memorable, as was the case in the bulls and bears example, but now let us consider a case where there appears to be fewer means of association and imagination.

In the stock market, there is a financial instrument called an option and you can either have a *call* option or a *put* option. The call allows you the right to buy some underlying asset, while the put gives you the right to sell that asset. Initially, many students get confused over which does what. 'Is it the call or the put which allows you to buy/sell the asset?' they ask. To make things easier, our lecturer once again gave us a brilliant way of remembering. When you think of a call, think of its first letter, C, being right next to the letter B, which can stand for *buy*. When you think of a put, consider the letter P and a nearby neighbour, the letter S. This can stand for *sell*. So what we then have is C.B. (*C*alls – *B*uy) and P.S. (*P*uts – *S*ell). Thinking of calls and puts in this way makes it easier to remember which of the two gives the holder the right to buy or to sell an underlying asset. Yet again, it may seem somewhat laborious to work out such associations, but if you exercise your imagination and find them, your memory will be enhanced.

The testing effect

While using your imagination to create associations will help you encode information in your long-term memory, you also need to be adept at retrieving it. One of the most effective ways of achieving this is by frequently testing yourself. This is something that many first-class students do. Furthermore, numerous studies in the field of educational psychology have shown that when students test themselves often on what they have learnt, they outperform those who merely restudy the material on which they are being tested. This phenomenon is known as the *testing effect* (Roediger & Karpicke, 2006). The mechanisms behind it are yet to be fully understood, but it appears that if you test or quiz yourself, the act of recalling information from your memory enhances the impressions already made in the brain. The analogy that is often used here is a footpath (Pete & Fogarty, 2007). If you walk across a patch of grass frequently enough, a permanent footpath eventually emerges. The same can be said of memory. Test yourself plenty of times and you will find it easier to retrieve the information you have learnt.

Summary

Memory masters are capable of remembering whole books, speeches and numerous conversations, word for word, with 100 per cent accuracy. As discovered in the 1982 study, these skills can also be attained by the average student, provided that they practise diligently using three key principles in the art of memory: association, imagination and frequent testing. It is these three principles that will help you attain memory mastery – a powerful ability that first-class students use to their advantage.

7

Task Management

Interview snippet

First-class student: Nishi Thakrar
Degree: Business Management
Institution: University of Birmingham

'In my first and second years, I paid attention to my work, extracurricular activities, as well as "play" (i.e. going out) and still performed well in both years. However, by the third year, I found it quite difficult to manage these aspects. I was also the president of a career-focused society, which became very time consuming. Therefore in the second semester of my final year, I handed over the position to the vice-president. I think that in the final year it is essential to have a very strong focus on studies and therefore this was my priority and the majority of other things became secondary. However, I still managed to meet up with friends three to four times a week and picked up on dance and going to the gym.'

A brief history of time (or clocks)

It is hard to imagine a time when clocks did not exist, a period when the concept of hours and minutes was alien to all. But there was once such a time. Despite primitive humans lacking sophistication, when it came to measuring and keeping time, they still managed to thrive on the simple notion of working during the day and resting during the night. Nevertheless, merely relying on night and day must have presented a number of problems. How could one, for instance, set off to hunt and return home, or meet with others, at a specific, prearranged time? To solve this issue, human beings required a more advanced way of regulating and directing life. As a result, the realisation that shadows changed length according to the position of the sun led to the invention of the sundial – a device that measures time using shadows and the location of the sun.

Invented by ancient Egyptians, sundials were later adopted by the Greeks and Romans in 263 BC (ICON, n.d.). As they became more frequently used (Ward & Folkard, 1996) and began to regulate with increasing detail and sophistication how and when we worked, some of those who were newly acquainted with these devices began to express their reservations. In one poem, for example, Roman comic poet and playwright Plautus complained about sundials. His argument was that this invention was governing how he went about his life. No longer was dinner dictated by hunger; now, the sundial decided when he ate. No longer could he rest when he was tired, because now the sundial decided when he woke up and when he slept (Mayall & Mayall, 1938).

Time management?

While Plautus's complaints are a slight exaggeration (you eat when you are hungry, not just because it is 7 p.m.), the modern world lies not too far from this notion. For example, 9-to-5 working hours are regarded as the norm and accepted just as much as we accept that the sky is blue. Generally, we work from when the clock says that we should start (9 a.m.) and stop when the clock says that we should stop (5 p.m.). Thankfully, though, university gives you complete freedom as to how you structure your day. Lecture and class times are the only elements that dictate your day-to-day activities; the rest is up to you.

The notion of time management often creeps up on university campuses in a misconstrued manner. While time management itself encompasses a wide range of activities such as organisation, planning and setting self-imposed deadlines, some students think that time management is all about deciding to spend a solid four hours studying, followed by two hours of rest and play, for example. Regardless of whether or not they have accomplished specific tasks, some students measure the work they have done by the hours they have invested as opposed to the actual tasks completed. Relying solely on such a notion has one result: you are not managing time, it is managing you!

I would therefore like to dispel the notion of working by the hour, for the hour, and replace it with the concept of *task management*. Here, a two-way relationship exists between time and work. Instead of relying solely on the hours to dictate whether you have studied enough, how about coupling this with the notion of setting goals to complete specific tasks, with a lesser emphasis on how long they may take? The idea of letting the work regulate the time as much as the time regulates the work is not new and in fact was recently packaged into a business management idea known as *ROWE,* an acronym that stands for 'results-only work environment'.

I came across ROWE in a peculiarly titled work by two former human resources professionals: *Why Work Sucks and How to Fix It*. Note that this is not about time management, but rather a book that presents the idea that in a results-only work environment, you are free to do whatever you want, whenever you want, as long as your work actually gets done (Thompson & Ressler, 2008). The book throws out the idea that we have to stick to strict office times and work schedules. Instead, it argues that in the workplace, productivity can be increased by as much as 41 per cent when a ROWE is employed.

Naturally, university is a ROWE (or rather, *ROSE* – a results-only study environment), because as a student you can do whatever you want, whenever you want. Nonetheless, many students forget this and often feel pressurised into sticking to a strict time schedule. If they have no schedule, they attempt to create a vague notion of time management. They build a schedule that they attempt to stick to with all their might, only to fail miserably and lose confidence in their ability to be disciplined. These are just some of the ills of poor time management systems. All they do is choke your freedom and autonomy.

When I was at university I employed a ROSE approach and reframed time management into what I call *task* management. The following section illustrates how this can be applied.

Applying task management

Universities have timetables of lectures and classes which you are expected to stick to, but as a student you are also free to design your work around these times as you see fit. The essence of task management is that you can do your work whenever you want to, just as long as it gets done. Below, I share some key ideas on how to manage the work you are assigned more effectively.

Plan

It is always a good idea to have a sense of direction when you embark on a piece of work. Aside from planning the actual content, you should also plan how you will complete the work itself. Here is something that worked for me that you could try: plan to break up your work into manageable, discrete tasks and set a self-imposed deadline to complete each of them. (For peace of mind, you should also have an overall completion deadline that is earlier than the one the university may have set for you.) Be sure to finish the mini-tasks before the self-imposed deadlines and put in however many hours it takes to do so. For example, if I had to write a 2000-word essay that was due in eight weeks, I would plan an outline and give myself, say, four weeks to finish it. Each week, I would allocate a day to spend on the coursework and aim to finish 500 words. After four weeks, I would have a completed essay with an extra four weeks left over to polish it, if need be.

However, with such a strategy you do have to allow for some flexibility. Given how often we underestimate the length of time it takes to complete certain tasks (Buehler *et al.*, 1995), it is wise to allow yourself additional time. This is because if your tasks are too large and the deadline you set arrives too quickly, you risk burning out if you keep working beyond what your body can manage. Therefore, the best thing to do is to plan for a task and set a deadline that has room for you to go over it. If you finish early, great! If you finish late, then at least you planned for a small buffer period.

Do

Once you have a plan with your mini-tasks, their mini-deadlines and an overall deadline that is earlier than the university-imposed date, you have to start doing the work. Be warned, though: procrastination will be waiting for you right after you make your plan. The only way to get past this evil is simply to start doing the work (we will touch on this again in Chapter 8). If you planned to learn a certain topic in a day, jump right into it even if you do not feel like it. If you must type 500 words, get on your computer and start typing whatever ideas come into your head. Also, be aware that studies have shown that the larger the task, and the more abstract it is, the more likely you are to procrastinate (McCrea *et al.*, 2008). To avoid this consequence, engage in your assignments in smaller chunks. Only then will it be easier to get started on the work than to procrastinate about it. There is more on procrastination in Chapter 8.

Rest

Doing your work depletes all manner of energy, so it is important to take breaks from it. While things like sleep matter more than you think (and I will touch on this later), here I would like to point out something that is perhaps less obvious: resting by indulging in some good old healthy fun. Yes, academic success involves a significant amount of self-discipline, self-control and willpower – things that separate first-class graduates from the average student population – but it is also important to let loose every once in a while. In fact, a number of studies have shown that self-discipline and self-control can be depleted (for instance Gailliot & Baumeister, 2007) and that in some ways, they are like a muscle. That is, they need training, but they also need rest. This is why in one study, people who had resisted the temptation of freshly baked cookies gave up more quickly on a subsequent problem-solving task than people who had had no prior indulgences to resist (Baumeister *et al.*, 1998).

So take a break from your work and do something fun. You just might find that when you return to your assignments, you can exert more self-discipline than if you were to work on them all day, non-stop.

Persist

Breaks aside (and this will seem contradictory), you should also persist with your work and aim to have fewer breaks and interruptions. Why is this? The answer can be found in psychology and behavioural economics. Dan Ariely, a professor in this domain, described a brilliant study in his book *The Upside of Irrationality*, where results showed that people suffered less when they did not frequently disrupt annoying experiences (Ariely, 2011). This is because we have the ability to adapt to experiences such that the intensity with which we experience them decreases over time. In essence, interruptions and frequent breaks from work can keep you from adapting to its challenging nature. I always found it harder to return to revision if I broke it up with too many breaks; I'm sure you have also experienced a time when you left work and found it harder to return to. So to 'suffer' less, attempt to tackle your work for extended periods of time before taking a break.

Finish

As with all things, moderation and flexibility will be beneficial when deciding when to stop working. In the final term of my final year, it was not unusual for me spend 12 hours in the library. I would not tire as quickly because the final exams were so close and the fear of failure and adrenaline kept me going. Nevertheless, when you do tire and reach a point where your study material hardly makes any sense, you must leave the task at hand and rest. Continuing with a tired body and mind is counterproductive. While the aim is to persist until a task is finished, if you underestimated how long it would take, you are better off readjusting your plan and finishing later.

Summary

The concept of time management is often misleading and can seem a little overwhelming. For example, a Google search for the term 'time management' produces over 100 million results. In this chapter, you were introduced to a much simpler concept that I used during my time at university: task management. The idea is about effectively planning and managing the tasks that are required of you and completing them in your own time, but well before university-set deadlines. Forget about the clock dictating your work arrangements; you are at university, not an office. Therefore, as long as you get your work done on time, it does not matter when you do it.

8

Procrastination

Interview snippet

First-class student: **Leona Nichole Samuels**
Degree: **English and American Literature**
Institution: **University of Kent**

'In absolute truth, prioritising was the only management tool
I used, and there were certainly times where my academics
were not a priority. For example, during my year-long tenure as
President of the Kent University African Caribbean Society, my
studies were absolutely secondary. There were also times in which
I was completing essays the night before their due date. Whilst the
superstructure of my academic style was perhaps erratic, there
was an infrastructure that established my success: attendance to
seminars and lectures, and keeping up with the reading. Those
two things are the growth factor for any student.'

A Severe Epidemic

How many times have you been assigned a piece of coursework only
to end up procrastinating for days on end because the task seemed too
large, or its due date appeared to be very distant? When nearing exams,
how often are you daunted by the amount of revision that needs to
be done, yet somehow you end up putting it off up until the very last
minute? My guess, if you are anything like me, is that this happens to
you more often than you would like. Everyone procrastinates. In fact, if
there is anything out there that is as good at bringing students together

as alcohol, it's procrastination. The epidemic is severe – many students report that procrastination occupies over one third of their daily activities (Pychyl *et al.*, 2000). Many of us feel helpless when it hits, and we never seem to learn how to beat it. Nevertheless, there is hope. By first understanding some of the root causes of procrastination, we can take a number of steps to combat it that I will share with you in this chapter.

The Causes

Procrastination happens for a number of reasons, among them the unpleasantness of a task, being overwhelmed and having no idea where to start, and, some argue, the lack of incentives to finish a certain piece of work. However, even with all the right incentives we often still fail. I had all the right incentives to graduate with a minimum of a 2:1 to secure my graduate job, but I still procrastinated, dare I say dangerously. It wasn't until I came across the work of Dr Pychyl, an associate professor of psychology at Carleton University and an expert on procrastination, that I realised part of the reason many of us are repeat offenders. In his short book *The Procrastinator's Digest*, Dr Pyschly points out that by procrastinating we are effectively avoiding the bad feelings associated with working (Pychyl, 2010). In the short term this is rewarding – for now, you enjoy a bit of relief and it feels good to put off that dreadful essay – but the guilt we know all too well comes later. The kicker, however, is that if you have ever taken a basic course in psychology, you will know from Pavlov's famous experiments that if a behaviour is rewarded, it is likely to be repeated. And there lies part of the problem. Not only do we procrastinate because a task seems unpleasant and daunting, we also take some gratification from the act of procrastinating itself. Fortunately, we can outmanoeuvre most of these shortcomings, even, in some instances, without having to employ too much willpower.

The cures

Just do it!

A key driver of procrastination, mentioned above, is that the work is simply unpleasant. As such, we put things off and somehow convince ourselves that come tomorrow, we will feel more like it. But you and I both know from experience that tomorrow can very easily turn into an ever-moving goalpost. We keep putting things off in the hope that there will be a perfect time when we are super-motivated and ready to do the work. Unfortunately, this 'tomorrow' never comes. The 'tomorrow' we end up getting is not one full of motivation, but one full of panic when all of a sudden an exam or a deadline is upon us. To avoid such a fate, you just have to get on with your work as soon as you practically can.

I know I am stating the obvious here, that when it comes to things you have to do, employing Nike's anthem *'Just do it!'* can save you a whole lot of heartache. But the obvious is not necessarily easily achieved and *just doing it* can be incredibly hard. However, if you keep in mind the expectation that you won't feel more like it tomorrow, you are likely to get on with your work right away. So don't wait on motivation and don't always expect it. Thankfully, it is entirely possible to become motivated after starting your work, especially as it starts to take shape and the pieces fall into place.

Be specific

As I pointed out before, another of the major causes of procrastination is not knowing where to start. Whether that is revising for an end-of-year exam, writing your dissertation or preparing for an interview, if you have no idea how you will tackle your work, you are more likely to procrastinate. I know this not only from personal experience but also from research, which shows that when presented with large abstract (or vague) tasks, we are more likely to procrastinate than when we are faced with more concrete tasks that have specific plans for how to complete them (McCrea *et al.*, 2008). So one of the ways in which you can beat procrastination is by breaking large and more abstract tasks into smaller, manageable chunks.

A personal example is how I managed to write this book. Initially, the notion of writing a book seemed vague to me. I spent many hours on Facebook instead of writing and for many days I procrastinated, because I could not figure out exactly how to start. But as soon as I had a plan and an outline of all the different topics I wanted to write about, the challenge became less intimidating. Instead of sitting down and saying, 'I am going to work on a 28,000-word project', I sat down and said, 'Today, I will aim to write 500 words.' I then went on to make it even clearer: 'Today, I will write 500 words on the topic of choosing a degree by comparing the hardest subjects with the easiest subjects.' Breaking down your assignments in such a manner should give you some more direction and enable you to take action.

Create positive associations

Studying and doing university work can be boring at times. So it feels good, at least in the short term, when we put the work off. Over time we may begin to associate procrastination with some kind of relief, but this, of course, runs contrary to what is best for us. Therefore, why not create some positive associations with the act of getting on with your work? One method I used extensively to work my way past procrastination was by promising myself that if I could get through a certain section of work, I would reward myself by doing something fun. The most effective example of this, I found, was to ensure that during term time I would do as much of my work on weekdays. This way, I could have all the fun I wanted to on weekends.

Of course, you don't have take such a macro view. You could combine it with a micro perspective. That is, on a day-to-day basis, you could decide that after 90 minutes of hard work you allow yourself a 20-minute binge on Twitter, Facebook or any other fun activity you can do between work sessions. Some people find that using a digital kitchen timer helps fight procrastination. The mere act of setting a specific amount of time to spend on a task can inspire you to get on with it and use the time you set yourself effectively. When the time runs out you can give yourself a treat. And by rewarding yourself every time you knock procrastination flat on its face, you will come to associate a 'just do it!' attitude with the good feelings that come not only from the mini-rewards, but also from the positive academic results that will ensue.

Distractions: The fuel of procrastination

In Chapter 11, we will look at how working alone can be more effective than working in a group. Part of the reason for this is that innocent banter might sidetrack your efforts. In this chapter, however, we are considering the broader topic of distractions. Student life is full of them and often they fuel procrastination. Instead of getting on with a piece of work, we check our Facebook notifications, spend ages trying to come up with a good status update, constantly ping away on our Blackberry phones, and spend hours on YouTube or random humour websites for entertainment. The number of things vying for our attention is endless and when a piece of work seems daunting and or unpleasant, these distractions lure us to pass the time while we try to muster up the courage and motivation to tackle the assignment at hand. How can we get such distractions under control in order to focus more on our work? The answer yet again is simple: distractions management.

The total elimination of some of our favourite time-wasting antics would probably lead to a very dull student life, so my advice here is first, to be aware of how much time you use up on such activities. Only by logging how much time I was on Facebook did I realise that I was spending literally tens of hours a month on an activity that added little value to my academic success. Secondly, actively manage the time you allocate to such activities. While I never eliminated Facebook from my life, I took a Facebook diet by temporarily deactivating it on the run-up to my final-year exams. I then reactivated it once exams were done.

The crux of distractions management is to block out the majority of distractions for a sustained period while you work. How I wrote this chapter exemplifies this method. The first thing I did was to log out of

Facebook. I then closed my email client and subsequently put my phone on silent. I locked the door to my room and decided that I was not going to give in to any of the usual distractions until I had completed half of the chapter. Only then could I put my phone back on, take a break or casually browse the web for a moment. Minimise your exposure to distractions and you will not only maximise your productivity, you will also minimise your propensity to procrastinate.

Summary

We procrastinate because we think we will feel more enthused about doing our work tomorrow. At other times it is because what is required of us is daunting and we have no idea where to start. And as we learnt in this chapter, we even draw some pleasure from putting unpleasant work off until the deadline hits us in the face. But for each of these causes there are pieces of advice that can help reduce procrastination. First, don't expect to feel more motivated on a tomorrow that may never come. Instead, get on with your work now. Secondly, break your work up into smaller, manageable chunks. Research shows that the more concrete a task is, the less likely you are to procrastinate about it. Thirdly, reward yourself a little every time you beat procrastination so that you make a positive association with the act of getting on with your studies. By employing these three ideas, in addition to managing the distractions that fuel procrastination, you will benefit from increased productivity and, ultimately, better university grades.

9

Lectures

Interview snippet

First-class student: Kimberley Hill
Degree: Economics
Institution: University of Nottingham

'When I had breaks between lectures I would go to the library and do the recommended reading for lectures I had had that week or the week before. If I had a short gap I would photocopy the relevant chapters so that I could read or highlight them at home. If I had longer I would read and make notes. I used my diary extensively so that I didn't get too far behind with the required reading, tutorials and essays. By doing this I always felt on top of things.'

Why you should go to lectures

Whether you loathe them or love them, lectures are a part of university life and are near impossible to do without. This method of passing on knowledge has been in use for around 800 years and I suspect that it will continue to be the main method of teaching for many years to come. Why should you consistently drag yourself out of bed at 8 a.m. to catch every 9 a.m. lecture? Or fight the urge to nap after a scrumptious and filling lunch to catch a late-afternoon two-hour talk? The reasons, while somewhat obvious, are often forgotten. For example, the most obvious of all is that you go to a lecture to learn what you are supposed to learn

(Dolnicar, 2004). Otherwise, how would you know what to study and what not to study?

Essentially, going to a lecture allows you to get some more direction on where you should focus your studies and lecturers will often emphasise this aspect. Furthermore, going to a lecture ensures that you will be exposed to all the important bits of information about your course, which your lecturer will communicate. Information such as the assessment criteria and how to get top marks is often shared in lectures. Another reason, though less obvious, is the social aspect of going to lectures. Just like school, you get to see many of your friends every day and, as mentioned in Chapter 4, this can do wonders for your happiness.

However, while going to lectures is important on your journey to a first-class degree, there are some failings, which we must address. In this chapter I shall discuss these issues, along with some possible remedies for them that can help you get more out of lectures.

Lectures – and lecturers – are not perfect

There were occasions when I felt I could achieve more with private study than by attending a long lecture on a sleepy afternoon. More often than not, I fought the urge to skip the lecture and attended anyway. While this was rewarding in some cases (for example, when a lecturer gave hints about what would be examined), in other instances it wasn't, partly because of the various failings and weaknesses of lectures. In a classic essay entitled 'Twenty terrible reasons for lecturing', Professor Graham Gibbs, a former director of the Oxford Learning Institute at the University of Oxford, went through a large number of studies that compared lecturing to other teaching methods. He found that while lectures can be just as effective as other methods, they are not superior (Gibbs, 1981). For example, unsupervised reading, he argued, may in fact be better than all face-to-face teaching when it comes to mastering facts.

Passivity and short-attention spans

Broadly speaking, lectures have four key failings for which I will provide remedies from a student perspective. The first is that they are largely a passive activity. Having someone talk at you non-stop for an hour or two is not always the best way to learn. In fact, research shows that students do better when they are more involved (Goodman, 1990: 24). Secondly, our attention wanes rapidly over the course of a lecture. The often-touted statistic by education researchers is that students have an attention span of roughly 20 minutes (MacManaway, 1970; Gibbs, 1987). Though this doesn't account for individual differences, it has some validity. As you and I know from experience, lectures significantly longer than this have an amazing ability to lull us to sleep.

Forgetfulness, individuality and pacing

Putting the above two weaknesses together leads us to our third failing, that information imparted in lectures is often forgotten quickly (Cashin, 1985). If you are not engaged and are too busy daydreaming, you simply won't remember much. I recall walking away from certain lectures asking myself whether I had learnt anything and the answer would at times be an unequivocal 'no'. In these instances I could easily have passed for a data point representing students who, in one study, only knew 8 per cent more about a psychology course they had taken four months ago than a control group of students who had never taken the course (Rickard et al., 1988)! Simply put, it is very easy to forget the content of lectures if you are not careful.

The final weakness to consider is that lectures do not cater well for individual styles of learning. Furthermore, they presume that all students will comprehend material at the lecturer's pace, which is of course not always true. Some students grasp concepts quickly while others take a little longer. This issue is very hard for lecturers to address, though it is often well remedied with tutorials and classes, which I would advise you always to attend.

Getting the most from lectures

Fortunately, universities are addressing most of these failings and whatever institution you attend, you will find that various innovations are taking place to make lectures more effective. While there is little you can do immediately to affect how your lectures are presented, I will share with you a number of ideas that can help you get more from your lectures.

Pre-read

One of the things I wish I'd done more of while at university was to prepare for lectures. On the few occasions when I actually did read ahead and knew what to expect, I kept pace with the lecturer. Also, I enjoyed seminars, which I did not normally like. Perhaps this has something to do with the fact that we usually enjoy things we are good at. Nonetheless, it's always beneficial to spend at least 10 to 15 minutes (30 minutes if you are keener) casually browsing over the next topic to be addressed. This way, if the lecturer's pace is too fast you will not lag behind too much as you will have already covered some of the content. Having done some pre-reading (which may or may not be mandatory) also means that you can focus on nuances of the lecture that may not already be in your handouts or other reading material (more on this later).

Take notes (and review them)

I have a friend called Tolu who always took extensive notes during lectures. While they were scruffy at best, they were detailed and extensive enough that many of my other friends were quick to borrow them whenever they missed a lecture. Even students who hardly knew my friend would ask for these notes in such instances. It should come as no surprise, then, that Tolu scored the highest average mark on graduation, won various prizes from the university and landed a place at the London School of Economics.

But is note taking really that advantageous? Well, the research says that it can indeed help. In fact, students who record lecture notes usually garner an academic performance edge over those who don't, whether they review the notes subsequently or not (Kiewra, 1985). And those who review their notes perform better than those who don't. What is even more interesting is that another piece of research found that students who missed lectures but borrowed and reviewed notes from a friend or the lecturer actually did nearly as well as students who had written and reviewed their own notes (Kiewra, 1991). So try to take a set of good notes at every lecture; if you miss one, find a student with a good set to borrow from. (Hopefully you already have study buddies who are willing to share their notes with you.)

Record lectures

Most lecturers speak at a pace of approximately 2 to 3 words per second, while the average student can only write at around 0.3 to 0.4 words per second (Piolat *et al.*, 2005). Rarely is it possible to write down everything the lecturer says. In fact, one striking study in the 1980s showed that most students only noted about half of the main ideas from a lecture, and less than a quarter of other relevant material (Baker & Lombardi, 1985). An easy way around this is simply to record the lectures. This allows you to listen to the lecture again either casually (while at the gym, or as you commute or cook, for example) or more formally, so that you can fill in the gaps in your lecture notes. Thanks to technology, obtaining equipment that can record audio versions of lectures is relatively cheap. You could, for example, use your mobile phone if it has audio-recording software.

Follow the spirit, not just the letter

As I hinted at earlier, you do not have to write everything down when taking notes. You can get more content from reading a book than from transcribing everything the lecturer says. Johann Gottlieb Fichte, a German philosopher who is among those who pioneered the modern form of lecturing, often mocked professors who could only regurgitate what was already on the page for all to see (Friesen, 2011). That is because up until the eighteenth century, the tradition had been to lecture on, or rather recite word for word, a given text when passing on knowledge. But with the advent of books and printing, the need to do so no longer existed. And so Fichte and others began to convey the 'spirit' rather than the 'letter' in their seminars. That is, they would lecture and add their personal comments and views. So when you go to a lecture, aim to pick up on such nuances, which are unlikely to be in your reading material. (Understandably, these nuances might be more evident in arts subjects rather than science subjects, where lectures tend to be less divergent and more logical and structured.) Of course, this is easier to do if you have done some pre-reading and have already covered the basic content.

Position yourself strategically

In my experience, I found that whenever I sat near the front I would pay more attention. I also made more of an effort not to fall asleep in especially long lectures. This is because I was too close to the lecturer for them not to take notice and call me out (I was always amused to see my peers embarrassingly named and shamed in this regard). Also, I chatted less to my friends because again, I was too close to the lecturer and did not want to offend them with my chitchatting. Since I was at the front, I also felt less self-conscious about asking questions and, as such, I contributed more in lectures. So in these instances I actually got more from the lectures.

I don't like sitting near the front. In fact, I prefer sitting near the back, or somewhere near the middle. But when it came to those lectures that I considered to be of particular importance (such as revision lectures), I would try to sit as near to the front as possible so as to motivate myself to take the lecture more seriously and pay more attention. My advice, therefore, is for you to sit where you feel most comfortable, whether that be at the front or at the very back. However, be willing to try different seating locations to establish where you get the most from the lecture. This might be down to a better a view of the lecture board or screen, a seat where you can hear the lecturer clearly or, if you are like me, a seat that helps you stay more attentive and less distracted by mid-lecture chats.

Summary

This chapter looked at why it is important to attend lectures. I argued that going to them could help you identify where to focus your studies and considered four key failings of the classic method of lecturing: the lecture's passive nature; our limited attention span of around 20 minutes; the ease with which we forget the lecture's content; and the inability of lectures to account for individual styles of learning. With these concerns in mind, I suggested a number of solutions. Reading ahead of the lecture should help ensure that you keep up to pace with the lecturer. Note taking ought to help keep you more active and attentive, as well as aid your recall. Recording your lectures should help you build a set of accurate and complete notes. Following the spirit of the lecture should lessen the need always to keep up with everything the lecturer says, while highlighting nuances that can propel you to higher marks. And finally, seating yourself strategically can contribute to increased attention and participation.

10

Body and Mind

Interview snippet

First-class student: Catherine Allen
Degree: Theatre and Performance Studies
Institution: University of Warwick

'I'm young enough to live by the work hard, play hard manifesto, and to some extent, that's what I did. However, getting at least seven hours of sleep is a mini-obsession of mine. It makes my days far more productive and enjoyable.

One thing that surprised me in the first year [of university] was how I was the only one who seemed to eat three meals a day. Everyone else seemed to have no rhythm to the way they ate! So eating relatively healthy food at normal times probably helped me be on the ball a bit more.'

Taking care of yourself

A healthy mind requires a healthy body. This means that in order for you to achieve your highest academic performance you should aim to keep fit, get enough sleep and have a healthy diet. In my final year, I got acquainted with the gym and frequented it three to four times a week. Spending time on the treadmill and lifting weights made the crucial revision period near the end of the year less monotonous and boring. I also always felt more energised after breaking a sweat and, in my experience, if your body feels good so does your mind. In this chapter I will reveal to you how taking good care of your body can give you a vital mental edge. But before we go on, just so that I don't get any lawsuits, always remember to consult a doctor before taking part in any strenuous physical activity.

Exercise

As I write this chapter I have just returned from a half-hour gym session. I find that physical activity helps me to relieve stress and maintain a higher level of mental stamina, particularly when I am preparing for an odious revision session, writing long essays or, as in this case, writing a book. Aside from the obvious physical benefits (who wouldn't like a great body?), scientific research is now revealing that there are many more benefits to be gained if you keep fit. Let us explore what some of these findings are.

Managing stress

The first of these benefits is stress management. Studies show that people who exercise at least two to three times a week experience significantly less stress than those who exercise less (Hassmén *et al.*, 2000). Indeed, there appears to be an inverse relationship between stress levels and physical exercise; that is, the more you exercise, the less prone you are to stress. While some people may attempt to use exercise as a means of releasing stress (I can picture someone destroying a punch bag after an upsetting event), it is important to note that studies in this area usually describe exercise as a preventive measure as opposed to a corrective one. So, while punching a bag may not necessarily make you feel better, taking part in physical activities could mean that you are less reactive to and recover more quickly from stressful situations. Also, studies show that cardiovascular exercise, in particular, appears to be the most effective stress reducer (Kravitz, 2007).

Increasing positive mood

The second benefit of exercise (and in particular aerobic activity) is that it has been shown to increase feelings of being in a positive mood while also reducing feelings of being in a negative mood (Kravitz, 2007). No wonder runners testify about a 'runner's high' after running long distances. One thing to note, though, is that studies in this area point out that benefits to mood are more likely to occur if you focus on personal improvement goals (Fox, 1999). So, instead of just going to the gym every week and taking on the same challenges, focus on running a little longer or a little faster, or lifting weights that are a little heavier. Achieving these mini-goals will raise your mood and build your confidence in your ability to grow and improve – a vital component in establishing the growth mindset discussed in Chapter 2.

Anti-depressive effects

The third benefit is that both cardiovascular and resistance (weight) training have been shown to have anti-depressive effects. In fact, in one study it was shown that 16 weeks of exercise training for patients with major depression was just as effective as taking the antidepressant drug sertraline (Ströhle, 2009). This does demonstrate, however, that the greatest benefits occur after a prolonged period. Doing exercise should therefore be something you carry on doing throughout your academic years, from the very beginning to the end and beyond. In my case, I still exercise to this day and intend to do so for as long as I can.

Reducing anxiety

The exam period may be one of heightened anxiety in which you have little time for anything else but revision. Nevertheless, you should keep on making time for some light to moderate exercise. This is because research shows that aerobic exercise can reduce anxiety and feelings of worry and unease. Again, the greatest benefits accrue to individuals who implement exercise as a more permanent fixture in their lives; that is, the greatest beneficial effects occur when you exercise for a minimum of 10 to 15 weeks (Kravitz, 2007).

Improving brain health

The final benefits relate to your grey matter. Though our understanding of the brain is still limited, several authors and researchers in the area of physiology suggest that physical activity may boost brain health and cognitive functioning (Kramer *et al.*, 2006). Findings indicate that regular exercise can improve working memory, multi-tasking capability and the ability to deal with doubt and uncertainty. Furthermore, it has been shown that aerobic exercise can boost creativity after just 30 minutes of exercise. This boost is also reported to last for at least two hours after a workout (Blanchette *et al.*, 2005; Bronson & Merryman, 2010), so hitting the gym before getting started on that essay could very well work in your favour.

Diet

In my final year I probably consumed around 100 chicken wings, 15 regular-sized pizzas, 60 cans of fizzy drink and, in contrast to the junk, only about 30 apples. My diet was far from perfect, but when I could, I always added in a bit of salad, drank lots of water and tried to avoid having fast food for dinner. As a student it can be very difficult to have a healthy diet because healthy food is usually more expensive than fast food, or it simply takes longer to prepare. While I am not a dietician – and I am certainly in no position to give dietary advice – science shows that junk food can negatively affect brain performance (Gómez-Pinilla, 2008). On the other hand, certain foods can boost mental capabilities such as memory and concentration. To benefit from this, try to see that your diet includes some of the following foods:

- ❧ Oily fish (e.g. salmon, fresh tuna) or walnuts and kiwi fruit: these foods are rich in omega-3 fatty acids, which can improve learning and memory (*Science Daily*, 2008).
- ❧ Fruit and vegetables: these contain antioxidants, which improve cognitive processing (thinking abilities; Zinczenko, 2009). They also contain a wide variety of vitamins and iron, which are all good for the brain.

 ☙ Water: your brain is 75 per cent water. For it to work at its fullest potential, it needs to be well hydrated. This ensures that nutrients are delivered efficiently and that toxins are eliminated. The better hydrated you are, the better your concentration will be (Stylianou, 2010).

I am not saying that to get a first you must become a diet freak; you don't have to. All the same, if you improve your diet, your mental capabilities can receive a boost. And if this boost is the difference between a 2:1 and a first, I see no reason why you shouldn't want to drink some extra water or eat extra fruit and vegetables.

Alcohol

Moderation is the key in alcohol consumption. In fact, research shows that as you age, moderate alcohol consumption is linked to enhanced cognitive skills and memory (Hanson, n.d.; Rodgers *et al.*, 2005). In other words, you don't have to abstain completely. However, do minimise binge drinking. A good drink from time to time may be fun, but you should note that long-term alcohol abuse could literally shrink your brain and cause severe neurological damage (NIAAA, 2004).

While these are the long-term effects, the more immediate concern for students comes in the form of hangovers, which may lead to you losing a full day's worth of focused work, maybe more, if you party too hard. Consequently, keep a watch on how much you consume and if you must binge, do so during the less academically demanding periods of the year, such as the first and second terms.

Sleep

I would be lying if I said I've never been up until 4 a.m., only to attend a 9 a.m. lecture the same day. And I am sure you can recall occasions where you went through something similar, perhaps getting even less sleep. I remember in one instance I spent a full 24 hours working on a piece of coursework that was due the next day at midday. I can tell you, it was far from pleasant and in the end I did not perform as well as I could have. Amusingly, my less than stellar performance is likely to have been a result of me being as good as drunk. This is because staying awake for 17 to 19 hours or more has been shown to impair our body and minds in the same way as a blood-alcohol concentration of 0.10 per cent (Williamson & Feyer, 2000; the legal limit for intoxication on UK roads is currently 0.08 per cent). Without enough sleep your cognition, memory and concentration take a hit. So try as much as you can always to get a good night's sleep. Doing so may even boost your ability to form insights – what researchers consider to be the building blocks of learning, creativity and discovery (Stickgold & Walker, 2004). If you are struggling with an academic concept, *sleeping on it* might be just what you need to solve the conundrum.

Summary

In this chapter we looked at how you can take better care of your body and, ultimately, your mind. To do this, find time to exercise and you will enjoy many benefits that spur you on to academic success. As well as exercising you should also attempt to have a healthier diet, minimise your alcohol intake and sleep enough. I have not offered any more detailed strategies here because some students prefer dance classes to a treadmill, others would rather have more fruit and vegetables than fish, while others may be able to get by on just six hours of a sleep a night, as opposed to the often recommended seven to eight hours. So find within these categories (exercise, diet and alcohol intake, sleep) a solution that takes into account what this chapter discussed, while also catering to your individual preferences.

11

Study Environment

> **Interview snippet**
>
> *First-class students:* Nishi Thakrar; Sabial Hanif
> *Degree:* Business Management; Economics
> *Institution:* University of Birmingham
>
> 'Overall, I prefer to revise and write essays on my own.
> However, I still found it useful to discuss material with others.'
>
> 'One of the things that contributed to helping me get a first
> was working with a set of people who are studious and perform
> well in exams. Not only will this push you to work harder to
> keep up with them, but it will also serve as a great source of
> knowledge in case there are things you do not understand.'

You don't have to study at home

I did 80–90 per cent of my academic work at university. I hardly ever
spent time at home working on coursework or revision. It was all done
on campus, simply because for me this was the best environment to
work in. It's like going to the gym. When I try to work out at home, I
don't feel quite as motivated and I end up doing a half-hearted session.
When I go to the gym, however, I feel more motivated to push harder
because I am in an environment where everyone else is sweating it out –
not to mention trying to impress the occasional attractive girl who ends
up running on the treadmill longer than I ever could!

It's often easier to be motivated in a gym environment. Likewise, it makes sense to find an equivalent environment for your studies. It is crucial that you find such a place, since it will be conducive to your academic efforts and motivation. Your home can be distracting at times (Xbox, television, friends, family). Therefore, my advice is that if this is the case, you minimise the volume of university work that you do at home and, instead, maximise the amount done in a more suitable environment. Home should be a place of rest, after all.

Let us now look at some of the considerations to have in mind with regard to a study environment.

Finding your study HQ

My favourite study area was a quiet zone on the third floor of the university library. There were a few desks near the window and this is where I sat almost every day for the intense six weeks that preceded my final-year exams. I loved this place. It had large desks, was quiet and had windows nearby for a fresh supply of air and sunshine. Also, my study buddies were usually on the same floor in case I had any queries. This was my study HQ and I was always more productive there than at home or anywhere else. You should also find yourself a study HQ in which to work. You may have to experiment a bit before you discover an ideal location, but once you do, you will experience a boost in your productivity.

An ideal study HQ will be a place with minimal distractions. It may also be among the most isolated places on campus. For instance, in my second year I tried almost every building, but eventually settled on the third floor of the university library because it was far from the communal area, and was quiet, distraction free and comfortable. Do note, though, that your study HQ does not have to be a university library. Any place where you can work comfortably for hours on end without distractions makes for a perfect location. If you live in a different city or country and want to revise in your holidays, you could also use a local library. Whichever location you choose, do as much of your work there as you can, so that when you return home you can rest and enjoy yourself.

Habitual attendance

The study HQ was like an office to me. During the Easter holidays I would be there from Monday to Sunday at 9.00 a.m. every day. At the end of the session (this was usually anywhere between 5 p.m. and 8 p.m.), I would go home and do no work whatsoever; I had the evenings free to do as I wished. This is a tip I took from Cal Newport, an accomplished MIT graduate and author of one of my favourite books, *How to Win at College* (Newport, 2005). The discipline and commitment required for you to go to your study HQ every day from 9.00 a.m. will only come through habit.

As a side note, your study HQ could become much like a second home as exams draw near. Though the first few days you attempt to go to your study HQ consistently will be tough, once you are a week or two into it, it becomes a habit and attending seems more natural. So much so, that missing a few days will be weird. As an example, there were times during my Easter holidays when I took a day off and it felt really strange. This is because I had got to a point where it was more natural to get up at 8 a.m. and shoot off for the university library than to stay in bed. Rest assured, if you can routinely go to your study HQ to work day after day, your academic performance will improve tremendously.

Flying solo

Many students love to revise in groups, but after three years of experimenting, I can tell you that this is not always as effective as working alone. Getting into groups produces all sorts of ills, mainly in the form of banter, that is often thought to be harmless. A casual chat here and there eventually adds up to minutes, and later hours, wasted on unrelated topics. Some might argue that in a group you can discuss topics and therefore learn faster (I agree), but imagine a situation where someone keeps asking questions and interrupting your flow as you study, or you interrupt the flow of other people as they work. Spending all your time studying in a group is a breeding ground for such disruptions. To minimise them, I would recommend that you spend a good chunk of your time working alone.

Do note that when I say 'alone', I don't mean that you completely lock yourself away from all your friends (remember, study buddies are important). Rather, at least find a space away from large groups of students. It is perfectly fine to have your study buddies or other friends working nearby. However, it is vital that you spend more time focusing on your individual work requirements. In my case, most of my study buddies worked on the same floor but, as mentioned in Chapter 5, we had an implicit code of conduct. We only got up to ask each other questions when we felt that we had absolutely exhausted all other means of attempting to find the answer. Only then would we interrupt each other. This was a sign of respect for each other's time and since interruptions were minimal, questions were always welcome and answers would be given freely. No doubt group work can be beneficial, but too much of it can slow you down. So as a rough guide, aim to spend 80 per cent of your time working alone and 20 per cent working in groups to discuss topics and ideas.

Summary

It is important to work in an environment that is conducive to your concentration, focus and productivity as you revise or work on a piece of coursework. In this chapter I suggested that you find a place with minimal distractions and that is quiet and comfortable. Make such a place your study HQ by going there on a consistent basis, much as you would with an office job. Spend at least 80 per cent of your time working solo and the other 20 per cent discussing topics and ideas with friends in a similar environment. Do the majority of your work at your study HQ and you should have little to no work to take home – a place where you should chill out and relax.

12

Coursework

Interview snippet

First-class students: Catherine Allen; Leona Samuels
Degrees: Theatre and Performance Studies; English and American Literature
Institutions: University of Warwick, University of Kent

'I think in any subject area it's really important to use your creativity in the work you do, as examiners and tutors probably love to be excited by something that's different.'

'As a Humanities graduate, there was always plenty of room for nuance and innovation. Memory was not very important, but rather the fresh connections you could make between texts at that given moment.'

Made to stick

In the summer before my final academic year, I came across a brilliant marketing book called *Made to Stick*. Up to that point, I had written my essays and worked on my coursework in a somewhat haphazard fashion. Somehow I always scored highly and if anyone asked how I did it, I found it difficult to convey my technique. On reading this book, however, I discovered what I had been doing all along. This chapter will detail the strategies and principles I used to attain high coursework marks and, ultimately, the highest dissertation mark in my year.

Coursework success

Made to Stick is about communicating your ideas in the most effective way possible – about how you can make your ideas *stick*. According to the authors, Chip and Dan Heath, your ideas stick when they are easier to understand, are more memorable and can inspire a change in opinion or behaviour (Heath & Heath, 2007). Imagine if your coursework had all of these attributes; you would no doubt get higher grades. When you are writing an essay, or any piece of coursework for that matter, you are essentially conveying an idea or argument. By applying the principles laid out in this section, your ideas will achieve a larger impact and this will ultimately result in higher grades.

 Made to Stick offers six key principles to help you make your messages more powerful: Simplicity, Unexpectedness, Concreteness, Credibility, Emotion and Stories. These form the acronym SUCCESs. While the principles are about ideas in general, I have adapted them in the manner in which I interpreted and applied them to my work at university. Social science and humanities students are lucky here in the sense that my interpretation of the principles is in a form you can most readily apply to your own coursework. For students of natural sciences or subjects that involve less essay writing and more lab-based projects, I would suggest that you still read the ideas but think of ways you can adapt them to the nature of your own coursework. I consider each of the SUCCESs principles in turn.

Simplicity

Be simple with your coursework – not simple in the manner of dumbing down, but, as the authors of *Made to Stick* suggest, simple in the manner of a proverb rather than a sound bite. For example, the proverb 'Money makes the world go round' is compact and has a deep, intricate message. One could literally write hundreds of thousands of words about the idea behind this proverb, yet the same message can also be compressed into just six words. Whenever I wrote my essays, I always searched for such elegance. Though my work was far from proverb-worthy material, the effort alone resulted in a level of clarity and simplicity that did not compromise the academic detail. This elegance almost always resulted in first-class marks.

But you may ask, 'How can I be simple in my coursework without dumbing it down?' Well, for one, being clear and concise in your writing allows you to eliminate superfluous ramblings that further complicate the ideas being communicated. Secondly, you can simplify without dumbing down by using *schemas* – a psychology term for anything that makes learning a new concept easier by relating that concept to something already known (very much like the association idea we encountered in Chapter 6). You could explain an atom by relating it to a solar system, for example, or you could from time to time use anecdotes or even well-known proverbs to illustrate an idea.

For instance, in my first year I was already applying the schema concept. In one of my first academic essays I had to answer a question on how the pursuit of one accounting concept was hampered by the need for another. To illustrate the difficulty of the trade-off, I started the essay introduction with the following Russian proverb: 'If you chase two rabbits, you will not catch one.' With it, I compressed a key idea in my 1000-word discussion into 10 words! In other essays, some of the schemas I used included diagrams, anecdotes and associations with other concepts. If you are unsure whether the use of such schemas is acceptable on your course, consult your lecturers and they will guide you on what you can and can't use.

Note that I am not saying that you should you litter your essays with proverbs; this could work against you. All I am saying is that if you have a complicated idea to discuss, find ways of making it easier to understand.

Unexpectedness

What has Jesus got to do with accounting? That is the first thought that went through the minds of the people who read the first chapter of my dissertation. Curious to learn more, they read on and the answer to the question was gradually revealed. When you write an essay, or produce some other form of coursework, always create something a little different to catch people off-guard and to pique their interest. This is what the concept of unexpectedness is all about. If a lecturer finds a piece of coursework that takes the boredom out of marking a hundred other similar essays, they are likely to reward the author, provided that he or she hasn't gone off topic and written material that is in no way related to the work at hand.

Concreteness

Concreteness is about bringing your ideas closer to your audience's world. It is about making the idea as tangible as something your audience can reach out and touch. *Made to Stick* rightly points out that the best example of concreteness lies in proverbs. 'Never judge a book by its cover' is easy to understand and to relate to because everyone knows what a book is. Those who frequently buy books can relate even more to the proverb because they have been through the experience of buying a publication with a great cover, only to find poor content inside.

To increase the impact of your ideas in coursework and essay answers, always remember to make them concrete. To achieve this, increase the degree to which the audience relates to your idea. For example, in one of my academic essays on the largest Ponzi scheme ever, I put the $50 billion figure that was swindled by Bernie Madoff into perspective by pointing out that this was approximately the GDP of Croatia, could fund the cost of the Iraq war to the UK ten times over, and was enough to build 60 new high-tech hospitals like one near my university. This made the figure more concrete and the reader could easily grasp its enormity.

However, concreteness is not just about putting statistical figures into perspective. With coursework, you must always make sure that you answer the question asked in as direct a manner as possible. When I was writing my dissertation, the greatest piece of advice I received from my supervisor was to make sure that I unambiguously stated my position and answered the question. Frankly, beating around the bush about where you stand on an issue will not get you many marks.

Another way to increase the concreteness of your answers is always to point out the direct implications that may affect readers or their world. For instance, though my dissertation was highly theoretical and abstract, in the final chapter I discussed the direct implications to the practical world. Make your coursework and essays more concrete by inducing such relatedness and you will be on your way to higher marks.

Credibility

Lecturers don't expect you, as an undergraduate student, to produce grand, new theories. However, they do expect you to draw from the literature in your subject area so that you form sound opinions and ideas. Referencing other established authors in your field is therefore the quickest and friendliest path to credibility – the notion of getting people to believe your ideas and arguments. It is no different from the music industry, where artists make their music more powerful by drawing on the artistic ideas of those who came before them. By way of illustration, the Grammy award-winning R&B singer Usher would not be Usher without Michael Jackson. Equally, Michael Jackson would not be Michael Jackson without James Brown. And James Brown would not be the same without Ray Charles.

To produce first-class coursework, you should draw from established names in your field and beyond, but without committing the ever-dreadful crime of merely copying and pasting. After all, if Usher were to imitate Michael Jackson 100 per cent, adding no new flavour of his own, his credibility would go down the drain and so would album sales. Authentic credibility is vital in all the work you produce. Invoke it by making sure that you are well read in your topic of discussion. Only then can you write with authority, citing when necessary from a number of reputable sources to support your arguments.

Emotion and stories

These last two principles do not necessarily go hand in hand. You can have emotion in your coursework without a story and sometimes – though it is less interesting – you can have a story without emotion. But what exactly is meant by emotion and stories? According to the authors of *Made to Stick*, emotion is what will get your readers to care, while stories are what will inspire your readers to act.

In my experience, you can get first-class results without utilising these two principles (hence I have coupled them together), but using them effectively can produce surprising results. In my degree (accounting and finance), the content gave little opportunity to evoke emotion as the majority of what we focused on was of a technical nature. However, such a limitation should not stop you from attempting to add a human touch to your work. One of the ways you can achieve this is by frequently asking yourself why anyone should care about what you are saying. This, of course, takes us back to the principle of concreteness; that is, finding the tangible implications of your arguments for the world of the person who is reading your work.

Summary

For nearly two years, I scored highly on my coursework without really knowing what I was doing. By the third year, and after reading a marketing book, I came to realise what I had been doing all along. I was getting first-class results in the majority of my essays because they were simple, had a touch of unexpectedness, were concrete, credible and contained stories and anecdotes. They all employed the SUCCESs strategy laid out in *Made to Stick*. Apply some or all of these principles in your coursework and you too will see a boost in your marks.

13

Exams

Interview snippet

First-class students: Mark Burton; Ibrahim Tolulope
Degrees: Master's in Mathematics; Accounting and Finance
Institutions: University of Manchester; University of
   Birmingham and London School of Economics

'I believe exams are largely about technique and memory.
To that end, I've always been lucky with a good memory
under pressure, which has helped me greatly.'

'[To revise] I get all the information about a particular
module on one A4 page and go over it in numerous
different ways. Teaching it to my younger brother helps
lodge it in my own mind, as well as talking about the
subject matter with friends and family.'

Exam strategies

Exams can be nerve-racking, but if you prepare sufficiently, the nerves
will be eased and your performance will be exceptional. This advice may
seem obvious, but it is amazing how many students end up severely
stressed because they did not prepare enough or properly. The tips
that I suggest below are simple – and perhaps you are already aware of
them – but when you implement them with a good work ethic, they can
produce wonders.

Plan your revision

Before you start revising, be sure to plan how you will tackle each module. You could employ the task management tactics discussed in Chapter 7, whereby you split module material into manageable chunks (or topics) and from there tackle each section bit by bit. Once you have a plan or timetable in place, allow for flexibility, however. This is because certain topic areas could take longer than expected or be completed earlier than planned. For my final-year exams, I went through three different revision timetables, mainly because I had underestimated how long it would take me to get through the key topic areas. Therefore, do allow for extra time in your plan in case this happens. If you happen to fall behind your schedule, don't beat yourself up over it; simply readjust the timetable and push on.

Start your revision early

As a general rule of thumb you should start revising at least four weeks before your exams. This is under the assumption that you have been keeping up with your lectures and are not going over material for the very first time. If you find yourself in the latter position – as I did in some instances – you might want to increase this period to anywhere between six and eight weeks. This will allow you additional time to comprehend the material before running through exercise questions and attempting to commit information to memory. Though there are students who start revising much later (in fact, a close friend of mine left his revision until the night before and still got a first, albeit with no sleep), your student life will be significantly less stressful if you allow yourself a comfortable amount of time to revise. So start early and save yourself the angst.

Make use of past papers

Past papers are often available to students, yet some choose not to use them or do so carelessly without a systematic approach. Indeed, past papers are like fire and, if I may quote George Washington without sounding too cheesy, 'Fire is a handy servant but a dangerous master.'

I say this because if you blindly follow whatever pattern you may have discovered in a series of past papers, you may end up being burnt. Many undergraduates are familiar with the experience of going to an exam only to discover that the questions they prepared for are nowhere to be found! This has happened to me and I am almost certain it has happened or will happen to you too. While past papers are useful for predicting future questions, they must always be approached with a degree of scepticism.

With that in mind, my advice is this: get hold of all the relevant past papers (your lecturers will usually tell you how far back in time you can go) and look for questions that come up frequently. These will reveal the most important areas in a module. Be that as it may, be sure to check them with the latest syllabus and also with your lecturers. By doing so you can ensure that the topics are still equally relevant. Once you have the main areas identified, focus your studies on them. You really do not have to revise everything. In scanning past papers, I always searched for the opportunity of not having to revise all the topics. Of course, it would be nice to revise everything (and you will definitely receive extra kudos for linking your answers between various topics, demonstrating superior overall module knowledge), but if you hone in on the core areas and master them, you can still get first-class results.

To sum up the above advice: (1) look for opportunities that mean you don't have to revise all the topics, by assessing the structure of the exam and looking at past papers to identify the key areas; and (2) for worst-case scenarios, insure yourself by studying a few back-up topics.

Practise under pressure

High-pressure situations can hinder performance. In sports, this is referred to as choking. It also happens in education. For example, when a lecturer puts you on the spot and asks you a question in front of the whole class, you might freeze up and not be able to answer it, when in other situations you could have dealt with it easily. The same also occurs in exams. I know of students who prepared maniacally but as soon as they entered the exam hall, the pressure got to them and they performed poorly. One way around this is to practise under exam conditions. Give yourself strict time limits and work through questions that you can mark and grade for yourself. You could also ask your lecturer if he or she has time to look at your answers and give you an idea of what grade you would have got. Only by practising under similar levels of pressure will you be able to deal more effectively with the real exams. Also, note that it won't always be practical to train using full exam timings. I actually practised most of my past papers using bullet-point answers. So save the wordy answers for a limited number of mocks and you will be able to get through many more past papers.

Understand first, memorise later

One of the most effective ways of committing academic content to your long-term memory is by understanding it first. Our brain finds it easier to remember things that have meaning, things that we can comprehend. In Chapter 6, we saw how an incomprehensible string of digits (you may test yourself here to see if you remember the 9-digit sequence) is easier to remember when you give it meaning. The same applies to academic content – you will find it easier to remember if you understand it. Spice it up with vivid imagery and imaginative associations and you can help further commit it to your long-term memory.

Notice that this relationship is circular; that is, to understand academic content you may employ associations with the already familiar (for example, the atom is like a solar system) and using associations in itself boosts your ability to remember. For this reason, understand first, and you will find that remembering is a no-brainer.

Power blagging

If for some reason you fail to understand certain ideas within a subject fully and are short for time, you may have to *blag it* in the exam. This, of course, is most applicable to essay-type exams, but it should nonetheless be an absolute last resort. If examiners see through your blagging, you can say goodbye to a first and say hello to a 2:2 or worse! But fear not, there are a number of steps you can take to increase your chances of appearing as though you know what you are talking about.

First, make sure that you are well versed in key terms and words that are commonly employed in the topic area. Using these words from time to time, and in the right context, will demonstrate some knowledge. Examiners usually look for key points when marking papers and if you can regurgitate key phrases or arguments in a valid way, then you will score better than if you didn't use them at all. Secondly, when power blagging try as much as you can to bring to your answer other relevant pieces of knowledge that you may already possess from other topics. Swaying an essay's direction to an area where you are more knowledgeable could provide a fresh perspective to an exam question and lead to better marks. However, always remember actually to answer the question.

Be flexible in the exam

Exams should always be tackled in a structured and disciplined manner, if you are to score highly. You should choose your questions carefully, structure and write your answers promptly (if you have essay questions you should do a real essay: introduction, body, conclusion) and maintain strict timing. Hopefully you will have planned all of this way before the exam so that all you have to do is follow through. A word of caution, though, as I have been preaching repeatedly: always be prepared to be flexible with your plans.

I remember one time going into an exam thinking, 'I will spend about 10 minutes reading through all the questions, pick the required four, and then spend about 40 minutes answering each one.' As it turned out, new ideas about certain topics emerged during the exam and I decided to include them in my answers. However, this meant that something had to give. The 40 minutes I had allocated to the other questions slowly dwindled down to 30 minutes apiece. As a result, I quickly had to re-edit some of the points and arguments I had prepared for the other topics. The moral of the story: be prepared to flex your planned answers, but only if the benefits of doing so outweigh the costs. Only take time from the other exam questions if you are sure that this will result in more marks. This brings me to my next point.

The law of diminishing returns

In an exam, the goal is to maximise the marks you receive for each question. If you have written all you can on a particular section and time is short, move on. There is no point attempting to write your way through to those higher marks when you have other unanswered questions waiting. This is because, as in many other areas, the law of diminishing returns applies. While this is just a theory (and I am sure you have experienced this, so it must be valid to a certain extent), many lecturers have corroborated it and I have experienced it many times, particularly on essay-type questions. It is always easier to get the first few marks on a question than to get the marks that reach out into the first-class zone. The relationship between time/effort and marks resembles this graph:

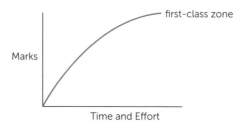

Clearly, this has implications for how you tackle your exams. For example, if you have four questions to answer (each one worth 25 marks), it is not worth spending a disproportionately larger amount of time on one question in order to get the full 25 marks when you can more easily pick up the first few marks on other questions. It may be easer to score 16, 16, 18 and 20, than to score 25, 15, 15 and 15, yet they both add up to 70 marks. Spending too much time on one question can result in you having less time to score the easy marks on the other questions. Therefore, if you find yourself focusing too much effort on one part of the exam, beware of the law of diminishing returns.

Summary

There are many ways to tackle exams, but in this chapter I have distilled the available methods down to a few key ideas that are the most universally applicable to various subject areas. Some of these include preparing early, making use of past papers and practising under pressure, understanding your course material, and using power blagging when you have to. If you employ these tips, exams will be less daunting and your performance in them should improve.

14

Concluding Remarks

This chapter contains three short sections on expectations; jobs and employability; and making the most of university.

Expectations

In your journey to a first, there are some things that you will not be able to control. You cannot control how lecturers mark you, for example, though you can work at your best to set yourself up for a first-class result. If you put in the effort, you will live without the regret of not having worked hard enough. However, understand that at times you may work hard and still perform poorly.

For instance, in my final year I remember working diligently on a management accounting essay during the Christmas break. But when I got my marks back I was shocked to see 54 per cent. This was an essay I had given my all to and yet here I was with a 2:2. Before that, I thought I had everything under control. I had even helped other students who were doing the same coursework get higher marks. What went wrong? When I got my feedback, I discovered that though the essay was well written, it did not address the issues the lecturer was interested in and, as a result, I had flunked 25 per cent of the module.

Things like this do happen. And to be honest, sometimes you will do everything in your power to perform well and you won't get the results you want. This is just the way life is. Sometimes it is a little unfair and our expectations are not met. Fortunately, when it comes to academic endeavours this is rare. More often than not, your results will be determined by the level of interest you have in a subject and how much effort you put in to do well. To get a first-class degree, expect to work hard, but if things don't go your way, understand that you did all you could and that is all that matters – knowing that you stretched yourself to levels you never thought you could reach.

Jobs and employability

When I graduated in 2010 we were just coming out of a recession and employers were a little more optimistic. In that year alone, employers recruited 17.9 per cent more graduates than in the previous year (High Fliers Research, 2010). In one way, I was lucky. The timing was perfect. Had I graduated a year earlier, during the credit crunch, or a year later, during the European financial crisis, I would have struggled to find work. Besides, the more vacancies there are, the better the chance of getting a job, right? Not quite. As it turns out, I wasn't that much better off because students who could not find jobs during the 2008/09 recession were now applying for the same jobs that new graduates were eyeing. It seems to me that whatever the state of the economy you will always be competing for jobs and that simply having a degree – even a first-class degree – in no way guarantees you employment after graduation. A great degree helps, but if you have ignored all other aspects of your development at university then you will find it extremely difficult to get a worthy job.

While this section of the book is no substitute for career services on university campuses, I will share with you three simple pieces of advice that have greatly improved the employability of countless university students.

Work experience

The best piece of advice I can give you to increase your chances of landing a job after graduation is simple: get work experience. This is by far one of the most influential factors when it comes to successful graduate job applications. The Graduate Market Survey of 2011 discovered that out of some 17,500 graduate vacancies, nearly a third (5,600 positions) were to be held for students who had prior work experience with the employer. In the most competitive industries (investment banking and law, for instance), up to half of the graduate vacancies were expected to be filled by previously employed students. Note that these figures are also backed up by a sentiment common among recruiters: when asked about the likelihood of a student with no work experience being hired, 60 per cent of employers in the survey responded that it was either not very likely or in some cases not at all likely (High Fliers Research, 2011). It is clear that given a suitable degree, the ultimate qualifier in getting a job is experience. I would therefore urge you to spend some time in a working environment, whether at a part-time job or in an internship related to a career of your choosing.

Forget perfect, be interesting

Acquiring 'employability skills' is often touted as one of the best routes to employment. Boring as it may sound, having employability skills is vital if you are to succeed in the working world. Aside from the more obvious specialist skills, which may be specific to a career in engineering for example, employability skills also include aspects like self-reliance, people skills and problem-solving abilities (HECSU, 2011). What is great about such 'softer' skills is that you can acquire them via an intent pursuit of your interests outside of academia. For example, at university I co-founded a t-shirt business with two friends. It didn't go far and we ended the partnership at the beginning of our third year. However, I learnt from it how to negotiate, how to lead and, most importantly, how to work in a team outside of traditional group coursework. Was the business perfectly successful? Not really, but it was an interesting and worthwhile pursuit that encouraged the growth of key employability skills.

You don't have to start a business to grow your softer skills, but with over 400,000 graduates leaving university annually (HESA, 2011), you cannot afford to attain employability skills in a way that is 'average'. If you have an interest, try to take it beyond what the ordinary student would do. Do you enjoy dance? Start a dance group and put on some charity shows. It will teach you how to motivate a team and how to organise and promote events. Are you a bit of a writer? Enlist at your campus university newspaper and doors in the media world are more likely to be open to you. You don't have to be perfect at any of these pursuits – you just have to try. Doing so will increase the likelihood of you emerging from university a more employable person.

It's a numbers game

When I started to look for internships in my second year at university, I initiated over twenty applications and did not get past the online application stage for many of them. I did, however, get a few interviews. This is where numbers help. The more interviews you can have, the better you become at them and the more comfortable you can be with the recruitment process. Not only are you increasing your chances by applying for more jobs, you also get plenty of opportunities to get better at selling yourself. Whenever I came back from an interview, I took plenty of notes and asked for feedback, which I could use in my next interview.

The worst interviews are often the best ones to learn from. I remember one that went particularly badly for me. It was a phone interview with a major investment bank. I was so nervous and intimidated by the process that I found it hard to string together coherent responses to the questions. While the interviewer was polite and friendly, she couldn't hire someone who could not communicate effectively under pressure (there are plenty of activities at university that can prepare you for this). Nevertheless, I learnt from the experience and did extremely well in subsequent phone interviews. Therefore, my last piece of advice with regard to employability is that you apply to as many companies in your industry of choice as possible. It will increase your chances of getting a job and also prepare and train you for the lengthy graduate recruitment processes.

Summary

A university education does not guarantee you a job. At best, a first-class degree may get you an interview, but from there, if you cannot demonstrate the ability to work with other people, for instance, then a candidate with a lesser degree and that ability will get the job. Fortunately, it is not that difficult to increase your chances of landing a graduate job. Get some work experience (it doesn't have to be a fancy internship), do something interesting while at university, and apply to plenty of jobs to ensure that you are comfortable with the recruitment process. Employing these three simple pieces of advice will be crucial to your success in the job market.

Making the most of university

Throughout this book, I have given you ideas and strategies you may employ to increase your chances of attaining a first-class degree or at least greatly improving your academic grades, drawing from both my personal experiences and some science. Having said that, throughout the book I have also attempted to stress the importance of achieving a sense of balance and flexibility in your student life. I absolutely believe that without this philosophy, my life at university would have been miserable and I would not have performed as well as I did. By getting a first-class degree without sacrificing your social life, and maintaining a mix of non-academic pursuits, you will graduate having made the most of your once-in-a-lifetime university years. You will also leave university with remarkably better employment prospects, as you will have become a more rounded person.

There is absolutely no need for you to slave away in the library, ignoring your other interests and social life just to get a first. This will make you boring, uninviting to friends and, ultimately, miserable. However, if you manage your work effectively and maintain discipline towards your studies while also conserving a life outside of books, you will find that university is much more enjoyable. In addition, when you graduate you can look back and say, 'I really rode those years until the wheels fell off!'

The Book in a Nutshell

In this section I summarise the key ideas in the book, chapter by chapter. This should serve as a useful reminder, once you have read the whole book, of areas that you might have forgotten about a few months down the road.

Degree choice

To get a first-class degree, ensure that you are on a course that genuinely interests you. It is also very advantageous to be on a degree for which you have some prior knowledge.

The growth mindset

Intelligence has been shown to be flexible. So believe in your ability to improve and grow, and you will find that you work harder and give up less easily.

Work ethic

Find something or someone that can inspire you to work to the very best of your abilities. Focus on your own development, but also ensure that your effort exceeds that of the average student.

Happiness and grades

Happy people tend to be more optimistic, resilient and, in some cases, even more creative. They also tend to get higher grades. As a student, don't ever ignore your happiness.

Support systems

Have you ever noticed how journeys seem shorter when you are with friends? This effect also occurs in other areas of life. A good network of friends, family and study buddies will help you manage the challenges of university more effectively.

Memory mastery

Your long-term memory has virtually unlimited capacity. To take advantage of this amazing feature and improve your memory, aim to use imaginative associations with what is already familiar as well as repeatedly testing yourself on what you know.

Task management

You do not have to be a time management freak. Simply set some personal deadlines for your work, break it into more manageable chunks and tackle it with less frequent breaks so that it isn't harder to return to at a later time.

Procrastination

No one is immune to procrastination. However, you can beat it by adopting a 'just do it' attitude and not always waiting for motivation. In addition, cutting down on distractions and ensuring that your work is designed to be less daunting (for example, by specifying a high-level plan for how to tackle it) can go a long way.

Lectures

The majority of first-class students attend most, if not all, of their lectures. They read ahead (not just the required reading, either), take notes and try to participate in lectures. Do all three of these things and you will take in more during lectures.

Body and mind

Your mind operates more effectively when you are taking good care of your body. So for superior academic performance, exercise, eat and sleep well, and avoid alcohol binges.

Study environment

It is important to find a place where you can study comfortably with a minimal level of distractions. For most students this is a library, but some prefer working elsewhere. Find such a place and use it as much as you can.

Coursework

Coursework is often about expressing and communicating ideas. If you do this well, you are more likely to get a first. So be sure to make your work elegant, creative and credible in order to attain top marks.

Exams

In most degrees, exams decide whether you get a first or not. So it is important that you are well prepared. Start revising early, use past papers and practise under exam conditions to ensure that you fulfil your potential in the real exams.

Acknowledgements

This book originated in an article entitled 'How to get a first-class degree' that appeared on my personal website on 17 July 2010. As I developed the idea into a book, Martin Phillips, a longtime school friend, helped me uncover numerous grammatical and spelling errors. Erika Davies, another longtime school friend, reminded me of the importance of keeping my writing voice clear and concise. I am grateful to these two wonderful friends for taking the time out to read various drafts of the manuscript.

I would also like to thank Suzannah Burywood for believing in the idea for the book and helping me improve the original manuscript to a level of quality I had not expected to achieve. Thank you, Suzannah.

Furthermore, I would not be where I am today were it not for my parents and the excellent support from my family. To them, I owe all of my past and future success. In particular, my parents have been a source of both inspiration and much motivation. I am ever so grateful to them and I hope to be a source of pride and joy to them for many years to come.

Last but not least, I would like to thank my study buddies and friends who provided an excellent 'support system'. You all know who you are.

Bibliography

Ariely, D. (2011) *The Upside of Irrationality: The Unexpected Benefits of Defying Logic at Work and at Home*, New York: Harper.

Aronson, J., Lustina, M.J., Good, C. and Keough, K. (1999) 'When white men can't do math: Necessary and sufficient factors in stereotype threat', *Journal of Experimental Social Psychology* 35(1): 29–46.

Aronson, J., Fried, B. & Good, C. (2002) 'Reducing the effects of stereotype threat on African American college students by shaping theories of intelligence', *Journal of Experimental Social Psychology* 38: 113–25.

Baker, L. & Lombardi, B.R. (1985) 'Students' lecture notes and their relation to test performance', *Teaching of Psychology* 12: 28–32.

Baumeister, R.E., Bratslavsky, E., Muraven, M. & Tice, D.M. (1998) 'Ego depletion: Is the active self a limited resource?' *Journal of Personality and Social Psychology* 74: 1252–65.

Birchall, M. (2007) http://business.timesonline.co.uk/tol/business/law/article1829803.ece, accessed August 2010.

Blackwell, L.S., Dweck, C.S. & Trzesniewski, K.H. (2007) 'Implicit theories of intelligence predict achievement across an adolescent transition: A longitudinal study and an intervention', *Child Development*, January: 246–63.

Blanchette, D.M., Ramocki, S.P., O'Del, J.N. & Casey, M.S. (2005) 'Aerobic exercise and creative potential: Immediate and residual effects', *Creativity Research Journal* 17(2 & 3): 257–64.

Bronson, P. & Merryman, A. (2010) 'Forget brainstorming', *Newsweek*, http://www.newsweek.com/2010/07/12/forget-brainstorming.html, accessed August 2010.

Buehler, R., Griffin, D. & Ross, M. (1995) 'It's about time: Optimistic predictions in work and love', *European Review of Social Psychology* 6: 1–32.

Buettner, D. (2009) *The Blue Zones: Lessons for Living Longer from the People Who've Lived the Longest*, Washington, DC: National Geographic.

Buzan, T. (2006) *Use Your Memory*, Harlow: BBC Active.

Carruthers, M.J. (2008) *The Book of Memory: A Study of Memory in Medieval Culture*, 2nd edn, Cambridge: Cambridge University Press.

Cashin, B. (1985) 'Improving lectures', http://www.theideacenter.org/IDEAPaper14, accessed August 2010.

CBS News (2008) 'Will Smith: My work ethic is "Sickening"', http://www.cbsnews.com/stories/2007/11/30/60minutes/main3558937.shtml, accessed August 2010.

Clore, G.L. & Palmer, J.E. (2009) 'Affective guidance of intelligent agents: How emotion controls cognition', *Cognitive Systems Research* March: 21–30.

Cohen, S., Doyle, W.J., Turner, R.B., Alper, C.M. & Skoner, D.P. (2003) 'Emotional style and susceptibility to the common cold', *Psychosomatic Medicine* 1 July: 652–7.

Croizet, J.-C. & Claire, T. (1998) 'Extending the concept of stereotype threat to social class: The intellectual underperformance of students from low socioeconomic backgrounds, *Personality and Social Psychology Bulletin* June: 588–94.

Daubman, K.A., Nowicki, G.P. & Isen, A.M. (1987) 'Positive affect facilitates creative problem solving', *Journal of Personality and Social Psychology* 52: 1122–31.

DeZure, D., Kaplan, M. & Deerman, M.A. (2001) 'Research on student notetaking: Implications for faculty and graduate student instructors, http://www.math.lsa.umich.edu/~krasny/math156_crlt.pdf, accessed October 2011.

Diener, E. & Biswas-Diener, R. (2008) *Happiness: Unlocking the Mysteries of Psychological Wealth*, Chichester: Wiley-Blackwell.

Diener, E. & Seligman, M.E.P. (2002) 'Very happy people', *Psychological Science* 13(1): 81–4.

Dolnicar, S. (2004) 'What makes students attend lectures? The shift towards pragmatism in undergraduate lecture attendance', http://ro.uow.edu.au, accessed October 2011.

Duckworth, A.L. & Quinn, P.D. (2007) 'Happiness and academic achievement: Evidence for reciprocal causality', Poster session presented at the annual meeting of the Association for Psychological Science, Washington, DC.

Dweck, C.S. (2006) *Mindset*, New York: Ballantine Books.

Elder, G.H. (1974) *Children of the Great Depression*, Chicago: University of Chicago Press.

Elder, G.H. (1998) 'The life course and human development', in W. Damon & R.M. Lerner (eds) *Handbook of Child Psychology*, New York: John Wiley & Sons Ltd, pp. 939–91.

Ericsson, A.K. & Chase, W.G. (1982) 'Exceptional memory', *American Scientist* 70(6): 607–15.

Forbes, C., Johns, M. & Schmader, T. (2008) 'An integrated process model of stereotype threat effects on performance', *Psychological Review* 115: 336–56.

Fowler, J.H. & Christakis, N.A. (2008a) 'Dynamic spread of happiness in a large social network: Longitudinal analysis over 20 years in the Framingham Heart Study', *British Medical Journal* 337(a2338): 1–9.

Fowler, J.H. & Christakis, N.A. (2008b) 'Social networks and happiness', http://www.edge.org/3rd_culture/christakis_fowler08/christakis_fowler08_index.html, accessed August 2010.

Fox, K.R. (1999) 'The influence of physical activity on mental well-being', *Public Health Nutrition* 2(3a): 411–18.

Fredrickson, B.L. & Branigan, C. (2005) 'Positive emotions broaden the scope of attention and thought-action repertoires', *Cognition and Emotion* 19: 313–32.

Friesen, N. (2011) 'The lecture as a transmedial pedagogical form: A historical analysis', *Educational Researcher* May 5: 95–102.

Gailliot, M.T. & Baumeister, R.F. (2007) 'The physiology of willpower: Linking blood glucose to self-control', *Personality and Social Psychology Review* 11: 303–27.

Gibbs, G. (1981) 'Twenty terrible reasons for lecturing', SCED Occasional Paper No. 8, Birmingham: SCED.

Gibbs, G. (1987) *53 Interesting Things to Do in Your Lectures*, Bristol: Technical and Educational Services.

Gómez-Pinilla, F. (2008) 'Brain foods: The effects of nutrients on brain function', *Nature Reviews Neuroscience* 9(7): 568–78.

Goodman, L. (1990) *Time and Learning in the Special Education Classroom*, New York: State University of New York Press.

Grant, M. (2006) 'Will Smith interview: Will power', http://www.rd.com/family/will-smith-interview/, accessed August 2010.

Guinness World Records (2011) 'First billion-dollar author', http://www.guinnessworldrecords.com/records-8000/first-billion-dollar-author/, accessed November 2011.

Haidt, J. (2006) *Happiness Hypothesis*, London: Arrow Books.

Hanson, D.J. (n.d.) 'Does drinking alcohol kill brain cells?' http://www2.potsdam.edu/hansondj/HealthIssues/1103162109.html, accessed August 2010.

Hassmén, P., Koivula, N. & Uutela, A. (2000) 'Physical exercise and psychological well-being: A population study in Finland', *Preventive Medicine* 30(1): 17–25.

Heath, C. & Heath, D. (2007) *Made to Stick*, London: Random House.

HECSU (2011) *What Do Graduates Do? 2011*, http://www.hecsu.ac.uk/research_reports_what_do_graduates_do_2011.htm, accessed December 2011.

HESA (2011) http://www.hesa.ac.uk/index.php?option=com_content&task=view&id=1974&Itemid=278, accessed December 2011.

High Fliers Research (2010) *The Graduate Market in 2010*, http://www.highfliers.co.uk/download/GMReport2010.pdf, accessed October 2011.

High Fliers Research (2011) *The Graduate Market in 2011*, http://www.highfliers.co.uk/download/GMReport11.pdf, accessed October 2011.

Holt-Lunstad, J., Smith, T.B. & Layton, J.B. (2010) 'Social relationships and mortality risk: A meta-analytic review', *PLoS Medicine* 7(7): 1–20.

Iannucci, L. (2010) *Will Smith: A Biography*, Santa Barbara, CA: Greenwood Publishing.

ICON (n.d.) 'Measuring time', http://www.icons.org.uk/theicons/ collection/big-ben/features/clocks-and-time, accessed November 2011.

Joint Council for Qualifications (2011) *A, AS and AEA Results Summer 2011*, http://www.jcq.org.uk/attachments/published/1575/JCQ%20 RESULTS%2018%2D08%2D11.pdf, accessed November 2011.

Kiewra, K.A. (1985) 'Investigating notetaking and review: A depth of processing alternative', *Educational Psychologist* 20: 23–32.

Kiewra, K.A. (1991) 'Note-taking functions and techniques', *Journal of Educational Psychology* June: 240–45.

Kramer, A.F., Erickson, K.I. & Colcombe, S.J. (2006) 'Exercise, cognition, and the aging brain, *Journal of Applied Physiology* 101(4): 1237–42.

Kravitz, L. (2007) 'The 25 most significant health benefits of physical activity & exercise', *IDEA Fitness Journal* 4(9): 54–63.

Kravitz, L. (2010) 'Exercise and the brain: It will make you want to work out', *IDEA Fitness Journal*, 7(2): 18–19.

Layard, R., Mayraz, G. & Nickell, S. (2009) 'Does relative income matter? Are the critics right?', CEP Discussion Papers dp0918, London: Centre for Economic Performance, London School of Economics.

Luria, A.R. & Bruner, J. (1987) *The Mind of a Mnemonist: A Little Book about a Vast Memory*, trans. L. Solotaroff, Cambridge, MA: Harvard University Press.

MacManaway, L.A. (1970) 'Teaching methods in higher education – innovation and research, *Higher Education Quarterly* 24: 321–9.

Marx, D.M. & Roman, J.S. (2002) 'Female role models: Protecting women's math test performance', *Personality and Social Psychology Bulletin* September: 1183–93.

Mayall, N. & Mayall, M.W. (1938) *Sundials: How to Know, Use and Make Them*, Boston, MA: Hale, Cushman & Flint.

McCrea, S.M., Liberman, N., Trope, Y. & Sherman, S.J. (2008) 'Construal level and procrastination, *Psychological Science* 19(12): 1308–14.

McKinney, R.A. (2002) 'Depression and anxiety in law students: Are we part of the problem and can we be part of the solution?', *Journal of the Legal Writing Institute* 8: 229.

Nadler, R.T., Rabi, R.R. & Minda, J.O. (2010) 'Better mood and better performance: Learning rule-described categories is enhanced by positive mood', *Psychological Science* December: 1770–76.

Newport, C. (2005) *How to Win at College*, Portland, OR: Broadway Books.

NIAAA (2004) *Alcohol's Damaging Effects on the Brain*, http://pubs. niaaa.nih.gov/publications/aa63/aa63.pdf, accessed August 2010.

O'Brien, D. (1993) *How to Develop a Perfect Memory*, Cambridge, MA: Pavilion.

O'Donnell, M. (2002) 'How to fight like Muhammad Ali', http://observer. guardian.co.uk/osm/story/0,641739,00.html, accessed October 2010.

Okinawa Centenarian Study (n.d.) *Okinawa's Centenarians*, http://www. okicent.org/cent.html, accessed August 2010.

Pete, B.M. & Fogarty, R.J. (2007) *Twelve Brain Principles that Make the Difference*, Thousand Oaks, CA: Corwin Press.

Pink, D.H. (2010) *Drive*, Edinburgh: Canongate Books.

Piolat, A., Olive, T. & Kellogg, A.T. (2005) 'Cognitive effort during note taking', *Applied Cognitive Psychology* 19: 291–312.

Powdthavee, N. (2008) 'Putting a price tag on friends, relatives, and neighbours: Using surveys of life satisfaction to value social relationships', *Journal of Socio-Economics* 37(4): 1459–80.

Push (2011) *Push National Student Debt Survey 2011*, http://push.co.uk/ Debt-Survey-2011-Headlines.htm, accessed November 2011.

Putnam, R.D. (2001) *Bowling Alone: The Collapse and Revival of American Community*, New York: Simon & Schuster.

Pychyl, T.A. (2010) *The Procrastinator's Digest*, Bloomington, IN: Xlibris.

Pychyl, T.A., Lee, J.M., Thibodeau, R. & Blunt, A. (2000) 'Five days of emotion: An experience sampling study of undergraduate student procrastination', *Journal of Social Behavior and Personality* 15(5): 239–54.

Rickard, H.C., Rogers, R., Ellis, N.R. & Beidleman, W.B. (1988) 'Some retention, but not enough', *Teaching of Psychology* 15: 151–2.

Riener, C.R., Stefanucci, J.K., Proffitt, D.R. & Clore, G. (2011) 'An effect of mood on the perception of geographical slant', *Cognition and Emotion* 25: 174–82.

Rodgers, B., Windsor, T.D., Anstey, K.J., Dear, K.B., Jorm, A. & Christensen, H. (2005) 'Non-linear relationships between cognitive function and alcohol consumption in young, middle-aged and older adults: The path through life project, *Addiction* 100(9): 1280–90.

Roediger, H.L. & Karpicke, J.D. (2006) 'The power of testing memory: Basic research and implications for educational practice', *Perspectives on Psychological Science* September: 181–210.

Rowling, J.K. (2008) 'The fringe benefits of failure, and the importance of imagination', http://news.harvard.edu/gazette/story/2008/06/text-of-j-k-rowling-speech, accessed October 2011.

Sager, M. (1998) 'The fresh king', *Vibe* 8(7): 130–36.

Schwarz, N. (2002) 'Situated cognition and the wisdom of feelings: Cognitive tuning', in L.F. Barrett & P. Salovey (eds), *The Wisdom in Feeling*, New York: Guilford Press, pp. 144–66.

Science Daily (2008) 'Scientists learn how food affects the brain: Omega 3 especially important', *Science Daily*, http://www.sciencedaily.com/releases/2008/07/080709161922.htm, accessed August 2010.

Scotsman (2003) 'The JK Rowling story', *The Scotsman*, http://www.scotsman.com/lifestyle/books/reviews/the_jk_rowling_story_1_652114, accessed October 2011.

Smith, S. (2007) 'The $4 billion man, *Newsweek*, http://www.newsweek.com/2007/04/08/the-4-billion-man.html, accessed August 2010.

Spencer, S.J., Steele, C.M. & Quinn, D.M. (1999) 'Stereotype threat and women's math performance', *Journal of Experimental Social Psychology* 35: 4–28.

Stickgold, R. & Walker, M. (2004) 'To sleep, perchance to gain creative insight?', *Trends in Cognitive Sciences* 8(5): 191–2.

Ströhle, A. (2009) 'Physical activity, exercise, depression and anxiety disorders', *Journal of Neural Transmission* 116(6): 777–84.

Stylianou, H. (2010) 'Brain boosting foods – boost exam performance', http://www.bradfordcollege.ac.uk/news-1/brain-foods-boosts-exam-results-1, accessed August 2010.

Thompson, J. & Ressler, C. (2008) *Why Work Sucks and How to Fix It*, New York: Penguin.

UCAS (2011) *Applications (Choices), Acceptances and Ratios by Subject Group 2010*. http://www.ucas.com/about_us/stat_services/stats_online/data_tables/subject/2010, accessed 2011.

Verkaik, R. (2000) '£100,000 starting salary as US firms lure legal talent', http://www.independent.co.uk/news/uk/crime/pound100000-%20starting-salary-as-us-firms-lure-legal-talent-706611.html, accessed August 2010.

Ward, J. & Folkard, M. (1996) 'Sundials', *New Zealand Garden Journal* 1(4): 16–19.

Willcox, B.J., Willcox, C. & Suzuki, M. (2001) *The Okinawa Program*, New York: Clarkson Potter.

Williamson, A.M. & Feyer, A.-M. (2000) 'Moderate sleep deprivation produces impairments in cognitive and motor performance equivalent to legally prescribed levels of alcohol intoxication, *Occupational and Environmental Medicine* 57: 649–55.

Zinczenko, D. (2009) 'Best and worst brain foods', http://health.yahoo.net/experts/eatthis/best-and-worst-brain-foods/, accessed August 2010.

Index